KEON
AND
ME

MY SEARCH
FOR THE LOST SOUL OF THE LEAFS

KEON
AND
ME

DAVE BIDINI

VIKING

VIKING
an imprint of Penguin Canada Books Inc.

Published by the Penguin Group
Penguin Canada Books Inc.
90 Eglinton Avenue East, Suite 700, Toronto, Ontario, Canada M4P 2Y3

Penguin Group (USA) Inc., 375 Hudson Street, New York, New York 10014, U.S.A.
Penguin Books Ltd, 80 Strand, London WC2R 0RL, England
Penguin Ireland, 25 St Stephen's Green, Dublin 2, Ireland (a division of Penguin Books Ltd)
Penguin Group (Australia), 707 Collins Street, Melbourne, Victoria 3008, Australia
(a division of Pearson Australia Group Pty Ltd)
Penguin Books India Pvt Ltd, 11 Community Centre, Panchsheel Park,
New Delhi – 110 017, India
Penguin Group (NZ), 67 Apollo Drive, Rosedale, Auckland 0632, New Zealand
(a division of Pearson New Zealand Ltd)
Penguin Books (South Africa) (Pty) Ltd, 24 Sturdee Avenue, Rosebank,
Johannesburg 2196, South Africa

Penguin Books Ltd, Registered Offices: 80 Strand, London WC2R 0RL, England

First published 2013

1 2 3 4 5 6 7 8 9 10 (RRD)

Copyright © Dave Bidini, 2013

Photos on pages viii and 154 from Harold Barkley Archives, courtesy Mike Leonetti.

Lyrics from "Subdivisions" (Lee/Lifeson/Peart) © 1982 Core Music.
Lyrics from "Finding My Way" (Lee/Lifeson) © 1973 Core Music.

Manufactured in the U.S.A.

LIBRARY AND ARCHIVES CANADA CATALOGUING IN PUBLICATION

Bidini, Dave, author
Keon and me : my search for the lost soul of the Leafs / Dave Bidini.

ISBN 978-0-670-06647-6 (bound)

1. Keon, Dave. 2. Bidini, Dave. 3. Hockey players—Canada—Biography.
4. Toronto Maple Leafs (Hockey team)—History.
5. Rock musicians—Canada—Biography. 6. Toronto (Ont.)—Biography. I. Title.

GV848.5.K47B53 2013   796.962092   C2013-902701-7

Visit the Penguin Canada website at **www.penguin.ca**

Special and corporate bulk purchase rates available; please see
www.penguin.ca/corporatesales or call 1-800-810-3104, ext. 2477.

FOR MY FATHER

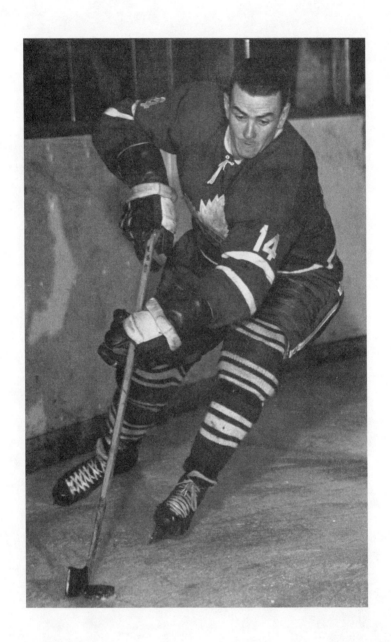

PART ONE

Growing up it all seems so one-sided.
—Rush, "Subdivisions"

1

The boy loved summer, but he loved winter more. The boy loved winter because it made him aware of his blood and his body and his heart, which pounded against the fabric of his snowsuit as he reeled into the rising clean of the wind and tumbling snow. As a man, he would understand what this said about the resilience of life and survival against the elements and other smart grown-up ideas about the world and the country where he was born—Canada, which is where Ontario is, and Toronto, too—but as a boy none of this entered his thoughts, which back then were shaped only by feeling and sound and smell and taste, the salty gross blood and sweet gross mucus creeping into his throat as he ran along the ice-thick streets with burning lungs and screaming knees and tired hands, the tennis ball rabbit-hopping over the snow-carpeted asphalt as he careered, lunged, fell, then sat for a moment with his stick, laughing at himself in the glorious winter sunshine, feeling alive while flowers slept and dogs curled into their fur dreaming of a world of slow cars and fat heavy butterflies.

The boy loved winter but he loved hockey more. The man can't remember when the boy first fell in love, but it must have happened before he was aware of it, sort of like evolution or God or the way a storm gathers over a part of the ocean that no one can see. The boy would have heard his parents shouting from the den or maybe their white-curtained bedroom with the big dressing mirror as they watched the black-and-white TV, the happy booming tenor of his dad and the twirling surprise of his mother's voice reaching him in the numbing twilight of a small dream. This love must have found him when he was awake, too, because a few years later, when his kindergarten teacher or aunt or neighbour asked him what his favourite colour was, he said "Blue," and while he wasn't sure why, the man would find out in time. The boy knew that it was a soft blue, home blue, city blue, Toronto blue, and he told the kindergarten teacher or aunt or neighbour that, too: "I live in Toronto." There was no blue on the black-and-white television and there was no blue on the newsprint of the *Globe, Star,* or *Telegram,* and there was no blue in the house, either, except maybe the rug in the living room, which is where they put up the Christmas tree every winter and where he took his first steps, although whenever his parents told other grownups about this it made him feel like a baby. The parks were green. The sun was golden. The team was blue and they were playing. There were voices; a man yelling through the speaker. Blue stripes. The *cack cack cack* of a stick. Then it was bedtime. More dreams.

Dave Keon became the boy's favourite player. He was the best player on the Leafs, and besides, he and the boy shared the same name, which was a big deal to anyone his age. The announcer on TV called him "Davey" Keon, but that seemed wrong. He wasn't like any Davey he'd read about in books or seen on Saturday-morning cartoons or heard about in Bible class at the church. Instead, Mr. Keon—it's what the boy would have called him if he had a chance to meet him, something he wanted to do badly but probably never would—wore a dark and serious look and was always hunched over whether he was skating down the ice or floating stick-at-his-knees into the faceoff circle. Mr. Keon had eyes like scissor blades and but a few sharp teeth; in fact, everything about Mr. Keon seemed angled in a serious, threatening way, even his sideburns, especially his sideburns. The boy wondered whether he would ever grow sideburns before deciding that he probably wouldn't, although no teeth, well, that was possible seeing as he lost them all the time. But if the boy's teeth had simply fallen out, Mr. Keon's had been the result of things that hurt: hard rubber patties spun at impossible speeds or a stick jabbed in anger or an elbow thrust at eye level winging down the ice. Unlike lesser players, whose faces had been drubbed into a mush of folds and fleshy scars, the boy thought Mr. Keon's had been carved to perfection, sharpened sharper, chiselled into a kind of rugged northern beauty. The boy also knew that the player was tough, not by what he did but by what he didn't do. During games Mr. Keon would often defuse a bad situation with an eye flicker, a scowl, a deep dark glare that gave opposing players sudden moments of weakness. The boy thought that impossible strength and the ability to fly and rubberizing your body like Reed Richards were all fine superpowers, but Mr. Keon's was the one he most wanted to possess: the ability to disarm an enemy not by laser or gun or clawed fist but by a look that said, Don't. Just don't. Not here. Skate away.

Mr. Keon wasn't mean and he wasn't vicious. He was just hard-working and strong, and hard-working and strong seemed to be enough. In a book called *Lowering the Boom,* written by that old player Bobby Baun, it said that whenever Keon would "stick his jaw out, you were never certain whether he was mad, or it was just [a] kind of determination," which may or may not explain how come, going into the 74/75 season, Keon hadn't been in a single fight ever, probably the only star player of his era to do this. Sure, there were fourth liners and sub defencemen and backup goalies who'd avoided getting involved this way, but never a player who'd taken a regular shift, let alone as team captain, a job that required standing up for and defending your teammates. But Mr. Keon did all of these things without dropping the gloves at a time when everyone dropped the gloves, fighting being a rite of passage in the 60s and 70s. Not even the terrible horrible Flyers could get Keon to fight and not even the big bad Bruins, who came before the Flyers. The boy knew as much about the NHL as anyone and he was almost certain that no one like Dave Keon had ever existed in hockey, although there was someone in life who stood for the same things, someone the boy had heard about in Mr. Caldwell's grade five class. The person had one name—Gandhi—and he looked less like a hockey player than anyone could have imagined: dressed in a bedsheet and sandals with little glasses and a small bald head. Mr. Caldwell said that Gandhi was in a war and that he refused to fight and because he did, people called him the saviour of India. The boy thought that being the saviour of anything was good, so Gandhi must have been pretty important. He was a superstar for not fighting back. Just as the captain was.

The boy thought that if Mr. Keon didn't fight, he wouldn't either, so even though Walter James sometimes bugged him—Walter was dadless and lived with his brother, Jimmy, and their mom on the bend of the boy's crescent—and other kids at school called him names because it's what kids his age did, the boy resisted scrumming with them or kicking at them or throwing punches because he wanted to be like his favourite player, although, of course, Mr. Keon was good at other things, too, which the boy wasn't, at least not yet. In a book called *The Leafs* written by someone named Jack Batten, Keon was described as the "perfect little centre," which seemed about right. Baun also called him "a whippet: small and quick," while Montreal's Andy O'Brien described him as "the will o' the wisp from Rouyn-

Noranda, one of the best little men in hockey." Keon was a good scorer in his peewee days, but was shaped into a great defensive player by a priest (of all people), a priest who liked to skate named Father David Bauer at a school called St. Michael's College (the boy wished the priest at his church could skate; it would make him less boring). After joining the Leafs, Keon was immediately asked to play against the other teams' best centres. He told writer Frank Orr, "In my first five seasons, I figured the only centres in the NHL were Montreal's Jean Béliveau and Henri Richard, Chicago's Stan Mikita, and Norm Ullman and Alex Delvecchio of Detroit." Because he stopped almost all of them from scoring, he earned a regular spot on the Leafs, winning the Calder Trophy as the league's best rookie. Later on he won four Stanley Cups, two Lady Byngs, two more with the WHA—the only player to win gentlemanly trophies in both leagues—and one Conn Smythe Trophy in 1967, the year the Leafs last won the championship. The boy could remember it happening, but only barely. People at a parade. Newspapers fluttering out of the sky. Men in fedoras and women in cat's eye glasses. Downtown. Microphones and laughter. The Chief. And then summertime.

In 1962/63, Toronto played Detroit in the league final. The boy's hero scored the winning goal in the fourth game with ten minutes to go against Terry Sawchuk, probably the greatest goaltender of all time. Keon left the ice under a barrage of Coke and beer bottles, Zippos, shoes, belts, keys, coins, hard-boiled eggs, and whatever else the Red Wings fans threw at him, but the captain didn't care. In the fifth and deciding game he scored twice, both goals coming short-handed even though the Wings defence focused almost all their attention on the mighty centreman. The boy had read something in a book by a man named Brian McFarlane (who was also sometimes on television) which explained how, despite his size, Keon was able to play through the hits and checks and blanket defence. The captain told him, "When they hit me hard, I roll with the check like a fighter making a heavy blow feel softer." The boy thought it made sense, and it reminded him of something the Leafs coach, Red Kelly, had once said: "Heck, if they can't catch you, they can't hit you."

The next year, in 1963/64, Keon did even more against a team that deserved to be defeated more than any other because they were almost always very good. In game seven at the Montreal Forum against the Canadiens, the Leafs won 3–1 and Keon scored all three goals—one short-handed, one on a power play, and one in an empty net—the single greatest playoff performance in team history. In 1968 Bugsy Watson, the shovel-faced enforcer, rejoined the Habs after a spell in Detroit, and when he asked his new teammates what had gone wrong in the previous year's final, they replied with a single word: "Keon." The small centreman—despite his core strength and mighty arms and legs, he was only five-nine and 163 pounds—was eventually elected to the Hockey Hall of Fame, making him the most decorated Maple Leaf ever. The captain had done almost everything in hockey. He was the greatest person and the greatest player and every day the boy woke up wondering if one day he would be like him.

If the boy loved summer but loved winter more, autumn was altogether different. Even though it meant the World Series and the CNE and Halloween and running across the front lawn before cannonballing into a pile of leaves, autumn also meant having to go back to school. Not only that, but in September, 1974—the year he turned eleven—the boy started at a new school, a middle school, which meant eating in a lunchroom instead of going home and walking a new route that would carry him to a place filled with kids from other parts of the neighbourhood, kids with strange names and different faces and funny teeth and weird hair in a building that was twice the size of any of their primary schools. Dixon Grove was so big that it made surrounding houses look like scotch-taped cardboard boxes. It had a great brown-brick facade and an enormous playing field and a scattering of portables beside the teachers' parking lot. It was three storeys tall with windows overlooking a busy street and long bright hallways high with voices and redolent of smells both sweet and terrible. There was a gymnasium and an auditorium with a stage and an office busy with people waving pens and shouting. There were photos on the walls of kids who'd gone there before as well as sports teams and old teachers who'd passed away. If primary school had been about playing outside and doing goofy word puzzles and learning math equations taught out of books with cartoon zebras counting multiples of five, middle school was about thinking and reading and listening to facts about a world that was far bigger and more complicated than the boy had ever imagined. If his primary school teachers—who wore flower-print dresses and had names like Ms. Drinkwater and Ms. Jollimore—taught them about God and Love and Heaven and worked to prevent the greater world from bleeding into their classrooms, the sandalled and ponytailed instructors at Dixon Grove wallpapered their classrooms with collages scissored from *Time* and *Life* magazines; Trudeau, John A. Macdonald, Martin Luther King, and Gandhi (him again) posters; a long poem by Alden Nowlan written in fancy script; a bullet-marked map torn from an *Esquire* folio that showed which countries had been to war and when; and scrolls with Joni Mitchell and Bob Dylan and "Dark Side of the Moon" lyrics. Coming after years of playtime days, Dixon Grove suggested that life was a long and ragged path rather than an arc that swept high into the air before safely coming to rest. Because this was a shock to the boy, he grabbed on to whatever he could to comfort himself through the changes: Mom and Dad and sister, his backyard, his room, his dog, his friends on the crescent. And the Maple Leafs. There were lots of things the boy didn't know, like how to do math equations with more than two steps; why adults liked beer and coffee even though they tasted terrible; whether or not pygmies existed and, if they did, how come they weren't eaten by cannibals; why girls liked David Bowie even though he looked like a girl himself; whether Captain America was based on an actual captain; how come his dog walked in a circle before sitting down on the floor in the basement; where poop went after it was flushed; and how come they let that awful smoking woman with the frilly shirt on television so much (it wasn't because she was funny). Through all of these mysteries of the world, there was one thing he knew for sure: Dave Keon would be a Maple Leaf forever. He was the captain. He wore number fourteen.

2

I used to love winter until the Leafs ruined it. Well, not all of it, but certainly enough of it. In the distant past, the first shimmer of snow once brought about feelings of hope and promise in times of cold and darkness, but after years of disappointment and sadness—and a few years after that—early evenings no longer meant running home at great speed or driving haphazardly through city traffic or willing the subway to move faster through the tunnel to get back in time for the game. Winter nights had me hoping the Leafs wouldn't play so badly that the thought of what I'd find in the next morning's sports pages made sleep difficult. Where the season once was bliss, now it was burden. Also: the flu. Frozen pipes. Broken car heaters and knees bruised after a fall. Ice. Salt. Traffic. There were other vagaries, too.

I learned to live with the pain, although, writing

that down, I knew it was a bullshit line. My pain wasn't the worst kind. It wasn't tragic relative to the world's tragedies, nor was it personally tragic. In fact, my life had largely been a series of untragedies, although like anyone I'd suffered and lost and been pricked by the hooked barb of fate. Still, I'd been relatively lucky. I earned a living doing what I loved to do—in fact, I loved it so much I'd never thought of it as a living, at least not in the conventional sense—and my family was fine and healthy and well balanced. Also, the winter yielded lots of good hockey, too, at least the kind played with my three men's teams and strangers at the outdoor rink. In fact, the only thing that wasn't fine or healthy or well balanced was that which followed me around like a sad tired bird floating across the topography of my life. The Leafs so imposed themselves that I wondered whether I would have traded in one of those other good things for the team to be less terrible (although, writing that down, I knew that was bullshit, too). Still, they were bad, had been bad, would probably continue to be bad. While this didn't hold me back from leading a good life, it didn't make it better. The team was my albatross and millstone, a heavy thing slumped across my shoulders that I was required, somehow by birth, to carry.

A smarter man would have changed NHL teams, would have sworn off his allegiance. I'd watched friends betray their fandom, choosing different sports entirely— in both cases, soccer—to fill the enormous vacuum created by the Leafs' futility. Many times I'd set out to make changes, only to be pulled back into terminal fandom the way a character in a sci-fi movie gets punted into deep space after the door to a spacecraft is pulled open. In fact, travelling through the nothingness and solitude of the universe wasn't far from what it felt like to be a fan. My allegiance was a black hole, a chasm, an existential crevasse. It weighed me down with its heavy emotional tar, and while some pitied my anger and sadness, most just shook their heads and laughed. I was a freak to those who didn't understand. Those who did compared miseries the way people who'd been to war or had come through poverty or had risen above illness talked about their lives. Still, if they were dealing largely with the past, others like me were chained to an eternity of suffering another bullshit line, but still. After writing these thoughts down in the late-evening quiet of my kitchen—a perfectly nice kitchen filled with perfectly nice things and the sound of perfectly nice people doing perfectly nice things in other perfectly nice rooms—I heard myself sigh. I decided to take a walk, but checked the radio first.

Florida, 1–0.

I swore and reached for my coat.

At season's end, it would be the eighth consecutive year the Leafs had missed the playoffs and the forty-third straight year they would not win the Stanley Cup, among the worst droughts in all of sports and the worst in pro hockey. A few years before, the Chicago Blackhawks had defeated the Philadelphia Flyers to win the Stanley Cup, their first in forty-nine years. The morning after their

victory, I shuffled downstairs in my pyjamas. It was early
summer and the hockey season was over. I pressed my
fists into my eyes, yawned, yelled upstairs for the children
to get out of bed—actually, that's a lie; my wife did most of
the yelling—and stood in the living room looking for the
remote. After finding it, I turned on the TV to find this
written on the screen:

LEAFS BIGGEST LOSERS IN HOCKEY

I harrumphed (this is also a lie; I don't really harrumph)
while continuing to weigh—I'm a weigher, it turns out—
what it meant to be a diehard fan of THE BIGGEST LOSERS
IN HOCKEY. Not only that, but THE BIGGEST LOSERS IN
THE BIGGEST MARKET IN THE BIGGEST CITY IN CANADA.
People talk about Cleveland's or Buffalo's or Seattle's
lack of pro sporting success but none of those cities are
considered the nerve centres of their game. Imagine
the Yankees not reaching a league final since 1967 or
Manchester United as the laughingstock of world soccer.
Actually, don't, because you can't. Recent victories by the
Blackhawks or Bruins only served to mock me, and others
like me. THE BIGGEST LOSERS IN HOCKEY. Right there.
Written on the screen.

I walked down the front steps and headed south. It
was early spring but warm, crocuses pushing too early
through the too-moist earth and yard birds singing June
melodies below April skies, which loomed snowless and
strangely pink. I wore an old ravaged blue hoodie with a

Maple Leafs crest stitched on the back, a crest that should have unsewn itself from the fabric by now but somehow had not. I felt loyal to the hoodie because it had survived nearly twenty years shelled over my head and torso, and besides, it was warm and softly lived in, if possessing traces of every scent through which it had ever passed, for better or worse. I gathered my arms in the hoodie's pouch, one hand finding the other through opposite sides. Moving down the street through the city—I live downtown, way downtown—I thought of the government and sex and money and kids and school and my column and music and sex and gigs—I'm a musician as well as a writer—but across that thought frequency Florida 1–0 dinged like a bell at an empty desk in a cobwebbed hotel staffed by no one. Florida 1–0 reminded me that the Leafs had fallen to last in their division, although I knew that was too common a description for what had happened. *Spiralled down* was probably a more appropriate way of putting it, but so was *tumbled from a great height,* although *pulled asunder and sucked into the void* and *collapsed under a great crushing weight* and *rotted from its historically fetid insides* and *forty men digging an enormous sporting trench into which they vaulted* also did the trick. After sitting in sixth place by Christmas—a position in the standings the team hadn't reached in a half-dozen years—the Leafs had won five games, lost sixteen, and suffered through a ten-game home-loss record, a new franchise mark. Their dramatic general manager, a large, florid Irish New Englander named Brian Burke who would be fired the next year, said that following the team's plummeting fortunes was like "watching an eighteen-wheeler going off a cliff." I wondered what lay at the bottom of the cliff. Since the team lacked any feel-good protein, the narrative of losing provided a strange kind of sustenance and, resigned to bad hockey, I craved the drama of failure the way a theatregoer relishes Oswald Alving in Ibsen's *Ghosts* admitting he has syphilis or the moment a Tennessee Williams doyenne goes mad.

I walked to the variety store. My boots dragged and made a sad slow sound along the sidewalk, even though, by nature, I am not an unhappy man. Then I heard a voice.

"I'm gonna fuck him up, bro. FUCK HIM UP!"

Four young men stood in an alcove ten feet ahead of me. Angry. Shouting. Tattooed. The angriest of them—eighteen years old, maybe nineteen—was frothing at the mouth, probably stoned on some new drug I'd never heard of and would never try. They were all wearing blue and white Maple Leafs sweaters—I saw two of them: KESSEL and PHANEUF—standing in a close, menacing circle made less menacing by the names of the players on their backs.

"I'd like to take a piece out of that douchebag," said the angriest one, grabbing the bundle of his crotch. He grabbed it hard. It looked like it hurt.

"Hahhahhh!!" shouted the smallest of the men, who wore a turned-around baseball cap with a Chinese character over the bill. They pushed their chests together and high-fived, laughing a mean, cackling laugh.

I walked closer to the men. Other times I might have

crossed the street, careful not to draw attention to myself. I might have pulled my own baseball cap over my eyes, or, feeling brave, smiled at them and said hello, trying to disarm them with kindness, although I did this far less than I liked to imagine. But this time I did something I hadn't done in ages, at least not since before the Leafs were an embarrassment and a humiliation. I walked closer still.

My relationship with the Leafs was abusive, like having a really bad boyfriend or girlfriend. They were the worst, most fatiguing partner in hockey, and because they were, I'd given up starting conversations about the team on subways and streetcars, buses and trains. Impressing upon people my sense of cultural insight, I used to opine, "The best way to connect with total strangers is to ask them if they saw the game last night. Ask them about the Leafs and you'll always get a response." But those times had faded. After a while these discussions were nothing more than a laundry list of complaints, both parties feeling upset that it had come to this. Rather than drawing people together, my favourite team had wedged us apart. The streets had fallen silent.

As I got closer, the kids looked up. I moved toward the angriest one, who had a neck tattoo, rings wound over his fingers, and two gold teeth patterned across his grille. He was smoking furiously. I showed the angry young man the fullness of my eyes, which reflected the sallow terrible pulp of nearly five decades of disappointment caused by the worst partner in hockey. KESSEL and PHANEUF and the angriest one stood in my path. They put their hands in their pockets, building a wall of blue and white on the sidewalk. I moved closer. And then I spoke.

"1–0 Florida."

"Ah, fuck," said the angriest one, shaking his head.

I also shook my head. "Fuckin' Leafs."

"Yeah," he parroted, "fuckin' Leafs."

They moved out of the way. I walked under the doorframe of the variety store and looked back to confirm that they hadn't jackbooted me in the alcove, burned my hoodie, and waved it like a flag, although I told myself that the idea of someone in a Leafs sweater beating me into submission would have been a poetic end to my life. The group stood together, the angriest one facing away. I read the name on the back of his sweater. I read it twice, then a third time. It gave me pause because I hadn't thought about the player's name in years. It was a good name.

KEON.

3

The boy lived in the suburbs. It was a new suburb, although not like the kind that would come later in the century with big boxes and malls and great paved subdivisions that left only a tiny parkette and a few woebegone trees. Instead, the area around the boy's house—a bungalow on a small crescent minutes from the main street, Kipling Avenue—gave way to ball diamonds and playgrounds, ravines and parks, all with steep embankments and a shallow creek that froze in the wintertime. It was easy for the boy's mom and dad to free their leash on weekends, knowing that if he wasn't playing road hockey outside the house, he was running across a soft forgiving green made softer still after a light snowfall. The boy's friends were the other kids on his street: the dadless James Boys—Walter and Jimmy—as well as Little Johnny, Guido Bertoni, Scott Carroll, and Frank Martello.

Sometimes, they rode their bikes to the Smoke and Gift at the Westway Mall, a tiny strip of stores with a bowling alley, shoe repair, pharmacy, music store, and diner. The Smoke and Gift sold *Hockey Pictorial* and the *Hockey News* as well as comics—*Cracked, Mad, Weird*—and some rock magazines: *Hit Parader, Creem,* and *Circus*. The shopkeeper kept dirty magazines on the top shelf—*Playboy, Penthouse, Oui,* and *Cheri*—and every now and then an adult took one down. The boy and his friends would stand there pretending to read *Archie*s and sometimes they'd see a boob pointing out from the pages or maybe even a photo of the girl's parts, which Jimmy James once called a beaver, something that made no sense at all.

In 1974 it was a given that almost everyone on the boy's street and in his class loved the Maple Leafs, although it's not as if the kids—mostly boys; girls didn't like sports as much—walked the hallways wearing their favourite logoed gear. Back then, loyalty to a team was expressed by different means because clubs didn't sell jerseys and hats and key chains and mugs and flags and seat cushions and foam fingers. There was a sporting goods store inside Maple Leaf Gardens—the arena where the Leafs played their home games—called Doug Laurie Sports, but they sold mostly hockey equipment—gloves, helmets, sticks, and skates—and only a handful of sweaters, charging extra to have the name of your favourite player sewn on the back. The only hockey sweaters the boy ever wore were his own—Vaughn Realty, BP Shell, Duke's Cycle and Sports—and even then he wore them only for games or practices, maybe a late-season team pizza party. Hockey sweaters weren't worn at school or in public. Back then, they were considered battle garments, warrior rags. You wore one, you played in one.

In the absence of three-hundred-dollar sweaters with players' names written across the shoulders, kids showed their team loyalty through hockey cards pasted to their lockers or pictures clipped from magazines and newspapers. Either that or kids sent away for autographed photos from the teams themselves of players posing with their backs slightly bent in full uniform standing over their sticks looking as if they'd never had their picture taken before, which, in most cases, they hadn't. The photos were made into postcards and slipped one after another into an envelope by a hennish assistant team secretary sitting at a small oak desk writing down the names and addresses of families from across Canada. One afternoon, the boy slid into the kitchen's yellow vinyl nook and, using careful penmanship on finely textured stationery from his father's basement office desk, he wrote the team asking for Keon and Salming cards. His mother folded the note into an envelope and walked it down to the post office. A month later, two pictures of Eddie Shack and Jim McKenny were delivered to him. They were okay, and certainly better than nothing.

The players on the Leafs were men and they had faces like men—cemented and established in their looks— while the boy's was still morphing, his features swelling then shrinking and moving about week to week. His hair was a dark shaggy stump that grew as if trying to pick a direction, blooming up and across in equal proportions. He had a face like a flat moon and eyes like acorns, and when he smiled his sockets creased on the outside, making him seem vaguely Asian. His lips were huge and bee-stung and his cheeks were for old ladies to pinch. One feature was more exaggerated than the next, and every time he stared in the mirror they seemed different, so who even knew what he looked like?

One of the first things the boy was required to do in grade six was tell the class what his interests were. Like every other kid, he stood at his chair speaking in a low quavering tone about how much he loved the Leafs and Dave Keon, the words leaving his mouth half-formed and too fast to be clearly heard. The boy's teacher was named Mrs. Reynolds and she stood at the front of the room smiling and nodding her head as the boy spoke then tried to sit down, only to be asked to repeat what he'd said, slower and more clearly. Mrs. Reynolds had warm brown eyes, a soft, creased face, and long hair that swept down her back. She called everybody by their first name in a deep and friendly voice that reminded the boy of that actress on *Bridget Loves Bernie,* the one with the buck teeth, although Mrs. Reynolds's teeth were normal, with a small gap in the front. She seemed like a nice person, and because she did, the teacher reminded the boy of his mother: kind and supportive, warm, understanding. When asked to repeat himself the boy tried to go slower, but his nerves made his speech even less comprehensible.

The only word that anyone could understand was "Keon," which, after he was finished, Mrs. Reynolds wrote in a great swooping cursive on the chalkboard. The boy saw that his teacher had strong hands, and, unlike his primary school teachers—who pecked with their chalk— she wrote in long, confident strokes, which meant that she could be trusted. After writing out the captain's name, Mrs. Reynolds drew a few strokes of light coming from the sides, like something from a comic-book script or maybe a movie poster. The boy liked his teacher even more.

The first person he encountered in class was a wiseacre named Phillip Zirko. Zirko was small with a hooked nose and messy hair. He was fond of Mrs. Reynolds, too, telling the boy, "The thing with her is, she doesn't look like she smells. All those other old teachers look like they smell. Take Mrs. Jamieson. Stinky. And more dandruff than Mount Everest." Saying that a person didn't look like they smelled was the closest Zirko ever got to giving anyone a positive endorsement. He sat in the back of the class and made sarcastic comments to anyone who'd listen. He once told Donnie Makem, "Is that your shirt or did someone puke on your chest?" and asked Ferdie Simmons, "What happened, Ferd? Did a lawnmower cut your hair?" Zirko had an older brother who fed him his best material, and even though the boy had to admit that his stuff was hilarious, Zirko sometimes made it hard for Mrs. Reynolds to control the classroom. During the first week, Zirko made a farting sound with his armpit after

John Peters bent over to pick up a book he'd dropped in the classroom. Peters was fat and had boy boobs and his family had come over from a place called "The United Kingdom," which sounded pretty important to the boy. After Zirko made his armpit fart, the boy laughed a loud, uncontrollable laugh, at which point Mrs. Reynolds spun on her heels at the blackboard and asked, "David, do you find this brand of humour somehow compelling?" The boy wanted to explain to her that, yes, of course he did—Zirko was as funny as Flip Wilson, maybe even funnier—but he felt bad for upsetting his teacher.

"No, I don't find it ..." he told her, not knowing what "compelling" meant.

Most of the kids in the boy's grade were normal with the exception of one person, Roscoe Nagy. The reason he wasn't normal was that he didn't like the Leafs. Instead, Roscoe liked the horrible terrible Flyers, and, although no one ever had the courage to ask him why, the reason that seemed clearest to the boy was that he looked like one of their players: tall and snaggle-toothed with pinched eyes and a caveman's brow. Roscoe's arms were a little too long for his body and vaguely dark fins of sideburn hair grew beneath his ears where, on most boys, there was only skin. Roscoe had a shaggy lead guitar player's mane—not quite Rick Derringer, but close—and wore brown leather shoes with a small platform, high enough at least to raise him above everyone else in the grade, including Russell Tyson, the high jumper, who was naturally as tall. His other features seemed merely smudged upon his face, cast, as they were, in a dark glow that wreathed him wherever he moved, broodingly, about the boy's school.

Roscoe possessed a few other Flyer qualities, too. The boy had heard that he'd been in several fights over the summer, and whenever he spoke it sounded as if the words were sour in his mouth; "gimp" and "fuckwad" and "dipshit" and "gearbox" and "faggot" stabbing the air like a sharp branch with a fish stuck to the end. Roscoe played hockey in the same house league as the boy and he was always running at other players the way the Flyers did, slashing kids and giving them facewashes. The coaches encouraged this kind of thing because of Roscoe's size and the effect he had on the ice, but the boy thought privately that he also skated as if burdened by his weight and height rather than propelled by them. The boy's team—Vaughn Realty of the Martingrove House League—had played Roscoe's team from Royal York, and whenever they were on the ice together the boy managed to steer clear of him, something he considered as great an achievement as whatever minor point totals he'd put on the board.

For the first few weeks of school, Roscoe lurked about the hallways—he was in a different class from the boy— but one Thursday after school, he cornered John Peters on the baseball diamond behind the building. By the time the boy and Zirko joined the crowd, Roscoe had already thrown Peters against the fence a few dozen times. The boy-boobed Peters was on all fours and crying—simpering really, although the boy didn't know that word—begging for Roscoe to give him back his watch, which, the boy

learned, had been a gift from his grandfather, a soldier
who'd fought in the Second World War. Peters's torn
Adidas bag lay like a small gutted animal near the pitcher's
mound, and in a moment of desperation the kid scrambled
to get it. Roscoe took two strides and planted a Kodiak on
Peters's back, pushing him flat to the ground. Most of the
kids stared while a few shouted at Roscoe to keep going.
The boy felt his stomach bubble with fear and excitement.
His heart raced and his bones grew hot.

"All right, gimp, you want your watch?" Roscoe asked
Peters, who looked up at him with his red face before
telling him that, yes, he did.

"Fine," said Roscoe, "then let's see you run the bases,
homo."

Peters pulled down his white dress shirt and
clambered to his feet. If his vaguely Yorkshire accent
and bright pink face and use of former boarding school
words like "portly" and "smitten" and "aluminium" hadn't
been enough to make him stand out among other kids—
words the boy would later learn were useful and good and
kind of interesting, although ones he wouldn't be caught
dead using in grade six—it was Peters's white dress shirt,
which he wore every day, that marked him as an outsider
and someone to be picked on. The shirt was torn at its
sleeves, and the boy thought about what Peters's parents
would say—what his own parents would have said—after
coming home with torn clothes, to say nothing of bruises
and a dirty face. The boy also thought for a moment about
Peters's grandfather, who'd fought in the war and maybe

killed Nazis and who'd given his grandson his precious keepsake, which Roscoe held in his hand as if he were about to squish a frog.

After Peters rose to his full height, the snaggle-toothed bully lunged at him, then pulled back at the last second only to see Peters drop awkwardly to his knees. Standing beside the boy, Zirko whispered, "What a little queer!" Roscoe told his prey: "On second thought, I don't want you to run the bases, gaylord. I want you to crawl them. All the way around."

Whether or not Peters could see the endgame, the boy couldn't tell. The fat kid moved on his hands and knees across the lime-dusted gravel, scraping holes in his dress pants as he passed around the diamond like a crippled Lou Brock. When Peters arrived at home plate Roscoe kicked his books to him and threw his bag against the fence, which the small British boy collected and gathered into his midsection. Roscoe turned to face the crowd, but the rest of the kids had quickly abandoned the scene. The boy was one of the first to leave, practically running the whole way home.

4

When I got back from the store, my daughter swept down the stairs and asked a question to which she already knew the answer: "So, how're the Leafs doin'?"

"Florida 1–0," I said.

"Shoot," said the girl, which was "Fuckin' Leafs" to a child new to the condition. I told her to hold on, then *shunked* the remote, the TV set revealing a new score blinking at the top of the screen: "Florida 4–1."

"Can I watch?" she asked, still believing, as I once had, that no lead was insurmountable and that the Leafs would come back if for no other reason than she loved them.

"Sure," I said, falling sideways across the chesterfield. I watched the game without actually watching it. Instead, I explored the feeling that KEON had engaged in me. I was loath to equate the feeling with hope. I'd felt hope before, lost hope before, had hope crushed before. But this was different. This was something three feet ahead of hope, lighter and quicker on its feet, wearing better shoes. The feeling reminded me of being a child watching the Leafs in the basement of my home in Etobicoke, my sister playing dolls in the corner, Mom and Dad sitting on the couch behind me. We were watching the Leafs, and it was okay, because there had once been a time when hockey in Toronto wasn't terrible. Instead of dreading games and being convinced of their outcome (always bad), we'd gather in front of the set almost certain that the Leafs would beat whomever they were playing, although probably not the Habs, and sometimes not the Flyers or Bruins, either. But it didn't matter. Back then, hope was founded on years of success as opposed to the possibility that something divine would happen and the Leafs would remarkably and impossibly win. I tried not to feel nostalgic about those times, but I didn't try very hard. Those times had existed. They were part of me and they were part of my city. KEON. He was the greatest Maple Leaf ever, and the first player I'd ever cheered for, maybe even the first person whose name I knew other than my mom's or dad's. Finding KEON on the thug's back at the bottom of my street on a Florida 1–0 evening: Was this some kind of a sign?

It was a wonder that any of my kids watched hockey. Last year my daughter said, "You realize that, ever since I've been watching sports, no Toronto sports team has ever been in A SINGLE PLAYOFF GAME!?" The girl was right. In eight years, neither the Leafs, Jays, Raptors, Argos, nor TFC had made the post-season. At first I'd protected them from knowing what they'd been born into, but after a while I couldn't help myself. A few years ago—feeling impossibly excited and hopeful (and naïve, of course) about the new season and wanting to generate enthusiasm within my home—I created a chart of the Leafs' schedule and hung it on the wall in the shape of a bottle of chocolate milk. I told the children that if the Leafs won two games in a row, they'd get a packet of jujubes; if they won three, they'd get a chocolate bar; if they won four, a bag of chips; and if they won five, a coveted bottle of chocolate milk. I did this partly to engage my son, who showed no interest in following the Leafs—proving wise beyond his years— and partly because it reminded me of being a boy cutting out the team's schedule from the newspaper and taping it to my bedroom door. The children chirped in delight at the appearance of the chart, asking: "Do you think we'll get our prize soon?!" I repeated the most hopeful yet hopeless phrase known to any fan who's ever supported a team out of habit rather than common sense: "It could be our year." The kids shouted "OUR YEAR!! OUR YEAR!!" as they ran out of the room.

After about six weeks, the chart fell off the wall. After about ten, it found its way into the closet, and after about twelve, it was carved up for birthday party name tags. That year—their year—the Leafs never won more than three games in a row—two Kit Kats and one Crispy Crunch was the bounty—and when I told friends and family what I'd done, they asked why I'd been so unnecessarily cruel. My wife had an answer at the ready: "Dave is just teaching them about dealing with pain and disappointment." It was a good line, but a sad one. My children would never grow up knowing joy and celebration and home-team triumph. They would have no Keon to celebrate. The Leafs would see to that.

I sat watching—but not watching—the game with my daughter. "Florida 4–1" became "Florida 5–1" and I realized that the last time I'd thought about Dave Keon was fifteen years ago, when, after being booked to speak at a literary event in a Chapters bookstore in the dark recesses of suburban Mississauga, I found myself grumbling down the highway before discovering at the other end that I'd be sharing the evening with Dick Irvin, the venerated Montreal Canadiens broadcaster. I had mixed feelings about Dick—his dad had coached the Leafs, but had also coached the Habs; in my eyes, a wash—and I wasn't sure about meeting him, let alone sharing an event. As I approached him through rows of chairs arranged for the evening's talk, the broadcaster appeared small and silver, his inimitable voice—nearly a parody of the quick-speaking pitchmen of his times—cutting through the store's rumblings.

The event's programmer introduced us and Dick Irvin said, "I hope we can talk a little music tonight," recognizing me as a guitar player and someone with whom he might kick back and forth opinions about big band music, the broadcaster's favourite genre, having hosted a show on Montreal radio for years. I pushed my hands into my pockets and said, "Hmmm. I was hoping we might talk a little hockey." I hadn't meant it as a joke, but it was taken that way. The broadcaster and the programmer laughed, so I laughed, too. Then Dick Irvin said, "So, you're a Leafs fan, eh?" I did as I'd always done—or usually did—whenever anyone brought up my weakness. I told Dick Irvin, "I really have no choice." Once again everyone laughed, even though once again I hadn't actually meant to be funny.

A few minutes before the event, Dick Irvin came over and poked the air, saying, "Dave Keon. Greatest Leaf ever." He then described an eyewitness account of what the Leafs centreman had done in game seven of the 1964 semifinal against Montreal in the Forum—how he'd singlehandedly taken apart one of the league's great teams in the most pressure-packed environment imaginable, scoring all three goals in a 3–1 Leafs win.

"Do you know how difficult that would have been?" he said. "How great a player he must have been?"

We were called to the front of the room. We read and talked to the crowd, although the old broadcaster did most of the talking. The evening was heavy with Habs lore, but it didn't ruin the occasion.

Years later, I met Dick Irvin a second time in Charlottetown, where I'd helped organize an event for CBC's "Hockey Day in Canada." Not knowing whether he'd remember me, I found him backstage and prepared to introduce myself. But the old broadcaster reached out and grabbed my hand. "Remember we did that event in Mississauga?" he asked.

After rolling that memory around in my head like a slow-melting caramel, I continued to think of Keon: how the captain hadn't played for the Leafs in thirty-seven years and had been in self-imposed exile, returning only a handful of times, the last being for an event in 2007. Keon had never forgiven Harold Ballard, the team's rapacious owner, who had assailed him in the press for not working hard enough on the ice to honour the club's legacy, which Keon himself had helped establish through the 1960s. At the end of Keon's contract in 1975, Ballard refused to consent to his demand for a no-trade clause, and when teams like the Islanders inquired about his availability—back then, clubs maintained perpetual rights to even non-contracted players—Ballard told them to stuff it, although he probably used worse language than that. While a compromise might have been at hand—the parties weren't far apart in money and Keon ended up signing with the WHA's Minnesota Fighting Saints for below what Ballard could have afforded—ownership provided no olive branch. Besides, some have suggested that the captain had long soured on the team's way of doing business, having traded away longtime Leafs like Bob Nevin, Dick Duff, and Andy Bathgate. Whatever grace and propriety former owner Conn Smythe had lent them was torn apart by the grotesque Ballard, an avaricious thug in a brown suit and ugly tie.

Lawrence Martin, who covered the Leafs for *The Globe and Mail* in 1974/75—Keon's last season—told me, "I loved the way the captain skated: slippery smooth, weaving in and out of the play and passing beautifully. He still had it that year—he was wonderfully talented—but his attitude changed. He'd become very surly and discontented and his teammates wondered what his problem was, why he was so angry and bitter. He no longer brought leadership and spirit to the team, something that had been a hallmark of his play in the years before. He seemed depressed for some reason. He was always short with reporters where he hadn't been in the past.

"During that season," remembered Martin, "there was a confrontation on the plane while we were flying out to L.A. [the road trip would end up being a disaster]. I'd been critical of the coaching as well as of Harold Ballard. Half the team was on my side, the other half wasn't. I had long hair and wore funny 70s clothes and a corduroy cap, so I didn't fit in with the old players." During the flight Keon seemed out of sorts, and at one point he told Martin that he didn't like what he was writing. He also told him, "You need a haircut. We might do it for ya." This was after a career of mostly avoiding the press, of the captain having maintained an unrippling effect on his team and their culture.

"In his last season, I got the sense that Keon couldn't relate to his teammates because he came from a different era," said Martin. "It was the 70s, but he had an old-fashioned mindset and the times were leaving him behind." Saul Korman, the Toronto clothier who grew up in Rouyn-Noranda, agreed with Martin. "When someone like Tiger Williams came up," he said, "it was all 'Fuck this' and 'Fuck that.' The language was changing—the times were changing—and I think all of this affected David."

Whatever the cause of Keon's discontent, his leaving gutted the Leafs of their emotional and spiritual centre, to say nothing of removing the one remaining connection to their last Stanley Cup team, for which Keon was named the Conn Smythe winner. Not only that, but Keon was the all-encompassing Canadian hockey player: Irish Catholic, bilingual, raised in Quebec, and playing for the Leafs. A handful of Anglos had skated for Montreal, but none were as mythic as Keon was to my city.

Remembering Lawrence Martin's words, I thought of something I'd read in a stack of old magazines I'd bought at a garage sale a few years before. So at the end of the Leafs game—Florida, 7–1—I descended into the basement looking for a *Weekend* magazine column written by Earl McRae, the pioneering Ottawa sportswriter. Tossing aside one paper after the next, I finally found it: a story composed on the eve of Dave Keon's induction into the Hockey Hall of Fame in 1986. McRae wrote that, in 1974, "an aging Keon was assassinated by a heartless owner. He was the Toronto Maple Leafs; they were him; and what followed was a cold and empty meaninglessness." Still, I wondered if what McRae was saying was this: having spurned the greatest player to ever wear their team's sweater, the Leafs doomed themselves to misery and failure evermore. I knew about sporting curses—it had taken the Red Sox eight decades to exorcise theirs, and after a hundred-plus years the Cubs were still damned—

and I asked myself whether or not Keon's estrangement meant that the Leafs were now suffering their own. Still, the Babe was long dead, while the Cubs' billy goat had fallen under the axe blade of some Byron Street butcher. Keon, on the other hand, was alive and well and playing golf. He had a tan and lived in Florida, or somewhere like that. You could reach out and talk to him, if only you could find him.

5

The boy loved hockey, but he loved writing, too. To him, there was nothing unusual about the dichotomy of these interests, although there was something unusual about the word "dichotomy," which sounded like what one contracted after swimming alone in a dirty African river. The boy loved writing because of how it made him feel: bigger and more powerful and more in command of his own body than he actually was, sitting, as he did, in the TV room downstairs, where he barely filled his father's wooden office chair, pounding away at the old metal typewriter that sat on his desk. Sometimes he wrote nonsense, and sometimes he wrote actual words and sentences, although they were usually nothing more than Leafs game reports and summaries of TV shows like the episode of *Sanford and Son* where Fred sells an ugly painting for fifty cents that ends up being worth ten grand. Still, the sound of the typewriter's keys chunking against the white paper produced a great noise that, from the first floor, sounded like a giant kicking a metal door, the boy's hands thrashing the air as his words stamped to life. In a way, the act was as physical as anything he did in sports, and after long writing bouts on weekend afternoons he'd drag himself upstairs feeling drained, sore, and exhausted. Years later, when the boy would become a man who would write in public places, he'd notice people watching him from café tables or library desks, possibly wondering if the computer would survive his keyboard punches, his body shouldered over the screen bruising out the words.

Because the boy loved writing and because he wrote a lot, his mother suggested that he try writing with a purpose. Of course, she didn't phrase it that way. She would have been more kindly and gentle-minded, holding a finger raised in the air, arrowing her eyebrows in thought and saying, "Wouldn't it be great to watch sports and write about them for a living? As your job?" One morning before the beginning of the 74/75 season, she noticed a section in the newspaper that published kids' writing—the *Young Sun*, a preteen supplement in the Sunday edition of the *Toronto Sun*—so she asked the boy if he wanted to submit something. Because the boy was only eleven, he didn't roll his eyes and say *ohhmygawwddmommm!* nor did he grunt or look confused as if she'd just spoken to him in Farsi. Bounding down the stairs to the typewriter, he jumped into the chair and tapped out an obvious word:

Keon

It looked great on the page, sitting there alone. It wasn't long, however, before the boy discovered that almost nothing rhymed with "Keon." One word came to him— "neon"—but after trying to fit some other words around it—*Look at Dave Keon / Shining bright as neon*—he laid his head in his hands, the first time in his young creative life that he felt defeated. The boy would grow up to be a man who would recognize what happened next as the very instant in which he became a writer, because, after wrestling with his thoughts for a while and very nearly wanting to walk away and forget the whole thing, he chanced to write down the name of another Leafs player, who wore a magenta top hat in public and rode around town in a dune buggy with the words POP SHOPPE on the sides:

Shack

The boy could have written about a lot of players on the 1974/75 Leafs. He could have written about Darryl Sittler, the tall, broad-shouldered, curly-haired centreman with the bashful smile and bullish stride whose gentle manner was belied by sudden gusts of rage that saw the softness of his youth harden like clay. He could have written about George Ferguson, the young idolesque pivot whose stick swept side to side in a pantomime of a farmer moving a scythe across a field. He could have written about Ian Turnbull—the dark-haired, wide-striding defenceman with the weighted slapshot whose wrenched, grumpy face reminded the boy of someone in a restaurant trying to send back his food—and he could have written about rookie Jack Valiquette, the slow giant of a centreman with a Musketeers' last name who seemed to stumble a little when he skated, but whose strength and ballast made it impossible for other defencemen to move him after he rooted his feet in the crease.

He also could have written about Bob Neely. Neely was a wild-eyed defender who moved around the rink like a dog running after a tennis ball and whose long furry sideburns looped below his ears like cursive J's. Before the season, the *Toronto Star*'s Red Burnett reported that three players—Tim Ecclestone, Errol Thompson, and Neely—had shown up for training camp "slightly bulging at the waistline." Neely, who was fourteen pounds heavier than the previous year, told the writer that "the delights of my new bride's cuisine" were the cause. Burnett remarked that in previous seasons Neely would have blamed it on drinking too much beer, but "the player says he climbed the wagon a month ago and plans on staying there." There was another mention of drinking in the same story and it involved the player whom the boy had decided to write about: Eddie Shack, the Leafs' rabble-rouser who had a wide swooshing moustache and a voice like an old woofing hound. Eddie was the team's clown, plonking other teams' tough guys from behind then pratfalling as if he'd been struck, drawing penalties and causing trouble. If Keon was the boy's favourite player because of his heroic nature and the way he carried himself on the ice, Shack was his second favourite because he was the funniest. He was nicknamed "The Entertainer." It made sense.

In a training camp report, Burnett wrote that "Eddie played the role of host at his golf club yesterday. He treated his teammates to a sumptuous spread after their annual golf tournament. Shack may bungle a few setups around a rival goal but he doesn't miss a crumb when it comes to putting on a steakfast" (reading the story, the boy thought that having steak for breakfast sounded both crazy and delicious and wondered whether this sort of thing existed anywhere other than at hockey team functions). The story continued: "When asked who won the tournament, Shack roared: 'Who cares? We only played about nine holes and everybody was having fun. You need this kind of break ... good food and a little schnapps ...'" The boy didn't know what schnapps was, so, a few days later, he asked his dad. "How do you know about schnapps?" his dad said. The boy told him he'd come across the word in the sports section. The boy's mom tittered when his dad said, "Well, that explains it," which didn't explain anything.

After the boy grew to be a man, he heard endless stories told by hockey people about Eddie Shack. Some of the stories were funny, and some were sad. One friend told him: "Once, just before a flight home from a game while playing with the Buffalo Sabres in the 70s, Eddie's ticket got upgraded. He gloated as everyone walked by him onto the plane. The plane took off and they shut the curtain to first class. Shack went into the bathroom, put on his bathing suit, and wrapped a towel around his neck. He soaked his head with water then walked shirtless into coach class, water dripping off him. He told the entire cabin: 'First class is unbelievable on this flight!'"

Another friend remembered that, as a child, he lived on the same street as Eddie, and it was a common occurrence to find him riding around the streets drunk on his ten-speed bike wearing a cowboy hat (Eddie had lost his driver's licence because of drunk driving). Sometimes, said the friend, "you'd see an evening's procession of silent, slow-moving cars following an illuminated Shack on his bike at the head of the procession." The friend added, "My mom always said that Eddie had 'boundary' issues. He'd wander into people's yards and pick fruit from their trees, go for a swim in their pool. In the morning my mom would walk the dog, and Eddie would be standing there in our backyard, eating cherries off our tree with a big grin on his face." Someone else told him, "One night I was wobbling home from the local pub when my girlfriend pointed out that Eddie was wobbling ahead of us. Before I could catch up to say something to him he'd swerved out of sight, and when we caught up to him and walked by, we saw that he was peeing against the side of his house. I hollered 'Hello!' and he waved back kindly, cowboy hat and all."

The man's favourite Eddie Shack story, however, was the one that took place right after the 1974/75 season, when a friend of his was hitchhiking back from Montreal during the transit strike. "One night," his friend remembered, "a pickup truck stopped to give me a lift, and when I opened the door, I saw that it was Eddie in his cowboy hat and boots. He asked me where I wanted to go. I told him and he passed me a beer. He took me out of his way, told stories the whole time, and I arrived safely where I had to go."

After typing Shack's name on the paper, other words came quickly to the boy: "back," "hack," "whack," "tack," "sack," "pack," and "track." Writing the poem was easy. He finished it within minutes and gave it to his mother, who folded the poem and tucked it into an envelope, which she addressed to the *Young Sun*. Two weeks later it turned up in the newspaper—on a page beside the comics, no less—and a few days after that the paper sent him a T-shirt: TO DAVID BIDINI FROM THE YOUNG SUN. It was the first time he'd ever been sent a free T-shirt—or a free anything—and the first time he'd ever seen his name in print. A few days later the season began and the boy was convinced more than ever that the Leafs would win the Stanley Cup. How could they not? The boy had written about them in the paper, and maybe one day he'd go on to write actual books about the team. The boy laughed when he thought of how conceited that made him sound. But maybe that was part of being a writer, too.

6

One of the problems with my Leafs problem was that, despite my frustration, disappointment, antipathy, and occasional anger, I still cared whenever the team showed even the slightest hint of progress or success: a promising first game by an unheralded rookie (Daniel Marois); a surprise shutout by an erratic goaltender (Peter Ing); or an inspired trade for a player whose potential, I convinced myself, would flourish the moment he was draped in Leafs blue (Andrew Raycroft). A previous evening's victory saw me bounce out of bed ready to attack the day while a loss slung like Houdini's padlock about my neck and arms. Whenever the Leafs fell behind I was drawn into a sullen, lightless cavern, while a goal scored by any player—good or bad, longstanding or short-lived, in pre- or regular season—immediately sugared the air, my body twitching in excitement. Once, I'd been watching a commercial where Leafs fans in different settings—a hospital waiting room, a diner, the stands of a neighbourhood rink—described the play-by-play of a last-second goal. The commercial ended with the GO LEAFS GO! chant looped over and over and the player scoring. With this, my arms shot into the air, knocking over a favourite lamp. As soon as my kids stopped laughing, they helped me gather the broken pieces, which we put on a dustpan and marched to the garbage.

Whenever—if ever—the Leafs won, I carried the feeling of victory around like a crazy person cradling a small beast—maybe a sickly bird or lamb—believing that, no matter how weak-bodied, my affection would be enough to rehabilitate the team through a transference of magical properties born out of unconditional devotion. In the end, wrong-headed management, lousy coaching, underperforming players, and bad karma would eventually kill it, drawing the last shuddering breath out of the wretched thing. Rare beasts who hung on and grew stronger—like teams from 78/79 and 92/93—hurt me even worse because their potential for success seemed real. The numbers proved this and the players were good, but like the rest, they could not avoid their fate.

Thinking about the time before this sporting darkness, the image of Keon sharpened in my mind: the brooding nature of his stare; the way his blade sat square to the ice like a cleaver on a cutting board; the smoothness of his stride turning choppy and quick whenever he was caught in small places; the almost inverse nature of his goal celebrations: raising a single glove into the air before hiding it as if embarrassed for having done something he shouldn't have, almost skating away rather than toward his celebrating teammates. His memory evoked an era of prosperity—or near-prosperity; I was only four years old the last time the Leafs won the Stanley Cup—and just reminding myself of it made me feel a little better. For the first time in ages I wasn't rigged to the team's pathos and tradition of despair. Instead, thinking of Keon lightened my perspective, and if I still felt the dampness of futility, I sensed that warmth and comfort would find me as long as I kept moving toward the captain, although I didn't know how or where or why or what for, not exactly, at least not then.

I asked myself why the angry young man had been wearing his sweater. Was it a hand-me-down from an older brother who'd been slain in a gangland shooting and had he worn it as a tribute to his fallen sibling? Had he found it wet and rumpled in an overstuffed bag of dead person's clothes left at the curb and taken it to warm the cool evenings? Or had the voice of his mother or father or grandfather stayed with him over the years, forcing him to honour the vintage Leafs captain after being told stories about how he played: fair and tough, yet defamed by management and driven away without saying goodbye?

Sometimes I rehearsed a conversation in my head that I imagined taking place in the air-conditioned cold of an American restaurant chain at midday in a strip mall near

Keon's home in Florida. The conversation finished with the player telling me how he wished I'd contacted him years before because things would have gone a lot more smoothly and the curse would have ended sooner. We stood up and hugged and I patted Keon's back. At home, a cloudburst of doves exploded over old Maple Leaf Gardens and sudden operatic singing filled the Air Canada Centre, the practising Leafs staring eyes-glazed into the stands as if in rapture. Children cried with joy and old women fell to their knees weeping. Open-line sports radio shows filled with callers lapsing into testaments of fondness for lamented players while transit workers waved riders through turnstiles. City councillors showed up for work in bunny-print pyjamas and the 1975 Philadelphia Flyers drove themselves to the city jail. Traffic stilled as men and women danced on car roofs. Forty-plus years of darkness were suddenly lifted.

Time passed—summer, and then fall—and with the coming of winter and another NHL season, the spectre of the old captain floated across my thoughts. For a while I worried that I was turning into an obsessive, like Richard Dreyfuss in *Close Encounters of the Third Kind* or that guy in *Zodiac* who finds himself chased around the city by the person he's meant to be chasing. I rooted around in my basement and found books from my childhood about the Leafs, shuffling the pages until I found photos of the captain in full stride, eyes ablaze—very nearly the Rocket's eyes—while curling around the net, one oven mitt held halfway down his wooden stick, the other holding off a player reaching in for the puck. I spent hours clicking through YouTube footage and even more time lost in towers of books tipped out of the Sports and Amusement stacks at the Toronto Reference Library. Wandering through the city, the number fourteen—Keon's number—stared at me from houses, ticket stubs, racing forms, and the weather channel. At the end of the day I lay in bed travelling back to when I was a boy watching my favourite player, triggering deeper memories of a childhood lost to the recesses of time: street hockey on Saturday mornings in my winter coat; eating lunch on Walt Disney World TV trays; the things I collected on the wall-sized shelving unit across from my bed (Muppets mug, stack of *National Geographics*, extra players from an old tabletop hockey game); the sound of the family dog breathing at my stockinged feet; the flight of my mother's voice as she called to me for dinner from the end of the long wallpapered hallway. A tiny wire chair my dad brought back from a trip away. My sister's Mick Jagger poster. Double pneumonia. The framed living-room watercolour of a single figure holding a fishing rod and standing in a boat. Sometimes, thinking about my boyhood left my guts in a terrible knot, making it impossible to sleep. Other times, I thought I might burst out crying.

While lost in this heavy emotional swirl, a friend called to ask if I wanted to go to New York City. The timing was perfect. I thought that a trip was what I needed to distance myself from the preposterous notion that I could somehow affect the team's fortunes by simply making contact with its former captain. Whenever I forced myself to measure this idea coldly, I was almost embarrassed by its pretension. They were the musings of a self-absorbed soul, I thought, whacking myself on the side of the head as if draining pool water from my ear. Still, this self-consciousness evaporated whenever the image of the kid's sweater found me. Jesus. Maybe it had fallen to me to take action after all.

I hadn't been to New York City in a while. The last time I was there I'd been sent by a travel magazine to write about the final season of Yankee Stadium. That trip, I saw two games, visited Monument Park, and tried to get into the press box, but because it was the park's last year, seats had been booked eight months in advance. I was left to sit in the stands without access to either the players or coaches, from whom my editor had requested quotes. I left the ballpark knowing that any story I filed would be inadequate, but because I was in New York City, I subwayed back into town and tried not to let it bother me.

I visited the Museum of Modern Art, wandering the exhibits in my fedora, long coat, and dark suit. At one point a small beatnik in a Van Dyke moustache standing beside a tall woman who looked like a young Yvonne de Carlo asked if he could take my picture. I asked him why and the beatnik said, "Because you, sir, are the most interesting person in this whole gallery." I must have looked surprised. The beatnik repeated himself, then added: "You remind me of one of those cool guys from

Vampire Records." I had no idea what Vampire Records was, but it didn't matter. According to the beatnik, I was the most interesting person in the gallery. It was good enough for me.

After wandering around town, I headed to the Film Forum on West Houston, where they were having a Robert Altman festival: fifteen movies screened over ten days. It had been a wet May, but that evening the rain stopped and the streets filled with people, making my promenade through the city seem exactly like what that word implied: bodies strolling about filling the sidewalk, pausing to take in every suggestion of what the new season promised, trees suddenly alive, city parks busy with a new pulse of movement, and lively voices pitched up and freed from thick parka collars and wool scarves.

As I approached the ticket window, I noticed a hand-printed sign taped above the wicket: TONIGHT'S FILM "THIEVES LIKE US" INTRODUCED BY JIM BOUTON. Q&A TO FOLLOW. I couldn't believe my luck. Bouton, the author of *Ball Four*, was a former New York Yankee who, in the winter of 1974, found himself acting in a film starring Elliott Gould (even better, Bouton played the villain) for one of the great American directors. Because he'd be at the screening, I thought maybe I could get my quote during the question period. I bought a ticket and a candy-striped bag of popcorn, and settled in for the show.

After the movie the crowd waited for Bouton, who eventually took his place behind a lectern rolled in front of the screen. Most of the questions were about Altman's

methods of directing, the circumstances that led to
Bouton's being in the film, what Elliott Gould was like,
and whether there'd been much rewriting on set (it was
all rewritten, according to the actor). I felt guilty having
to ask a baseball question in a crowd of cinéastes, but I
put my hand in the air anyway. The pitcher pointed to me,
and I asked: "Since they're tearing down Yankee Stadium
and moving across the street, I wonder, Jim, if you have
a favourite memory of the old ballpark." The pitcher
said, "I'm really glad someone asked me about Yankee
Stadium." I tried not to feel too taken with myself, but
seeing as I was also the most interesting person in the
Museum of Modern Art, this was, you know, hard.

Bouton's story was gold. He talked about his first time
pitching in Yankee Stadium, in the second leg of a two-
night double header in 1962. He remembered getting
to the park at 7 a.m. thinking he was the first to arrive,
only to find longtime trainer Gene Monahan preparing
the room for game day. Bouton went out on the mound
and stood in the empty park, imagining what he might
be doing in a few hours. He was racked with nerves, but
when it came time for him to start, he did, striding across
the field tall, sickly green, and wearing new pinstripes.
He walked the first three batters he faced, immediately
loading the bases.

"Manager Ralph Houk had one foot on the top of the
dugout the entire first inning," said Bouton. "I remember
going 3–1 on the fourth batter, then throwing a letter-
high fastball that the umpire, thank God, called a strike.

I got that batter, then got the next one to ground into a double play. I think I ended up walking eight batters and winning the game. Afterward they asked Ralph Houk about me and he said, 'Well, if Bouton keeps pitching the way he does, by June we'll have to get a new bullpen.' The relievers were up and down the whole game, but I stayed out there until the end. After doing an interview, I went back into the clubhouse where the team had laid a runway of white towels from the dugout to my locker. Mickey Mantle was putting down the final one just as I walked in. That was my first game in the majors."

I thought it was a great story, the very kind one should expect to hear in New York City. I wondered if, on this next trip, I'd hear other stories that would distract me from my own, although the nature of my visit made that unlikely. After all, my friend had wanted me to come to New York to sing "O Canada" at a dinner honouring Wayne Gretzky. The room would be filled with hockey players. I spared a moment to wonder if any of them knew the captain.

The dinner was held in an old converted Dutch bank across from Grand Central Station, in a restaurant called Cipriani—named for the famous Venetian restaurant and run by the same family. The classic room had enormous columns and floors inlaid with marble filigree. It was draped in velvet tapestries and bathed in red theatre lighting. The head table promised Brendan Shanahan and Gary Bettman as well as Pat LaFontaine, Senator Ken Taylor, Doug Weight, Ken Daneyko, Bob

Nystrom, Garth Snow, and Frank Mahovlich, whom my wife and I had met leaving his hotel to get to the restaurant across the street. As we crossed city traffic, I asked Frank's wife, Marie, about a recent visit to Moscow, her first after travelling to Russia for the Summit Series in 1972. She told us they'd gone to the Bolshoi, where an enormous buffet had been served between acts. "No one could have possibly eaten everything they'd put out," she said. "In '72 it was all so different. In the subway, I gave a small girl some chewing gum. She dropped the gum, went to pick it up, and a policeman came over and stepped on the girl's hand."

Before the dinner a reception was held in a room off the main hall, its curtained entrance patrolled by a young blond woman holding a clipboard. Beyond the curtain, I found Gretzky standing in a corner of the room horseshoed by fans, most of them young financiers and lawyers from Manhattan, and some of them ex-players: Jean and Denis Potvin, John Davidson, and Bill Torrey, the former New York Islanders GM. Gretzky moved effortlessly among them, shining through the fog of attention.

If I'd grown up wanting to be Dave Keon, I spent the better part of my young adulthood resenting Wayne Gretzky. Wayne was too blond, too pretty, too good. Too quick with a smile. Too GWG, too Leif Garrett, too perfect. And too many league records (it didn't seem right for one person to have so many all for himself). There was a time when I would have argued that Keon was a better—or at least more complete—player than the

Brantford wunderkind, but given the Leafs' fading legacy and the fact that Keon's absence had put him at the edge of the hockey firmament, it was hard to gain any support for my conviction. Still, as I waited for an audience with the greatest player who ever played, I couldn't help thinking that the person I wanted to meet most was down in Florida, resentful that he'd ever pulled a Leafs sweater over his shoulders.

As I approached him, Gretzky's eyes fell on my vintage 70s *Hockey Night in Canada* blazer: a gift from Dennis Ellsworth, the grandson of Jack Dennett, who'd performed with me onstage. Wayne pointed and said, "Hey, it's Don Cherry!" I told him, "Well, sort of." Talking to Gretzky proved easy and gratifying. A photographer showed up, gesturing for my wife and me to stand next to the player. I moved beside Gretzky, but he joked, "No, hold on, that's not right," shaking his head and laughing. He moved my wife into the middle and said, "This is how it should be." Gretzky seemed like a good guy. Only a small corner of my heart still felt melancholy.

After about twenty minutes, it was time for the crowd—about five hundred people—to assemble in the hall for the beginning of the event. My wife and I stood to the side of the stage, quietly strumming "O Canada," which wasn't a tricky song, but one I was loath to screw up, especially in front of so many guests, many of them large, their arms taut, hands gnarled, faces puck-bitten. Things became even more complicated when I noticed Mark Messier—"My God, he looks like Agamemnon," said my wife from a distance—whom I could ill afford to upset, making me feel more like Vladimir Kovin than I ever could have imagined.

We were introduced by Darren Pang, the former goalie. Before the event I'd told him that I was terrified of forgetting the words, but he just said, "You wouldn't be the first, and you probably won't be the last." It made me feel a little better, so, climbing onstage with the head table at our backs, I figured that if things went horribly wrong, I could somehow make them right. The crowd stood, and we started singing. The anthem sounded good and within a few moments it was over.

As I walked offstage with my guitar I turned to my right, wanting to acknowledge Gretzky, the evening's honoured guest. I also wanted to show him that the guy in the Don Cherry jacket had been me, singing the anthem. Instead I somehow looked the opposite way over my shoulder toward the other end of the dais, where my eyes fell on someone I hadn't noticed earlier standing at his chair. It was Leonard "Red" Kelly, the old pink-faced Maple Leafs coach, wearing a tweed jacket and beautiful Canadian tartan tie. I nodded at him. The old coach nodded back.

Red Kelly's career had produced two, perhaps three, marks of distinction. First, he was the only player to win eight Stanley Cups who never played for the Montreal Canadiens. Second, he'd been an all-star defenceman with Detroit—winning four titles with Howe, Lindsay, and Sid Abel—before becoming a Cup-winning centreman with the Leafs: a remarkable positional transformation. Just as importantly—at least to me— Kelly had run the Leafs bench throughout the mid-70s, nurturing stars like Sittler, McDonald, Williams, Salming, Turnbull, and Palmateer, as well as Keon in his last years with the team. I wondered if Red had kept in touch with the captain, having also played with him in the 60s. Maybe he knew where he lived exactly and why he'd stayed away for so long. I thought it would be crazy to come to New York and not ask him.

Growing up, I'd been devoted to Red Kelly's methods. In one sense, he was traditional and sober-minded, but in another, he was playful and kind of wiggy. I remembered Kelly wearing enormous brown bow-ties and having bizarre new ideas about how to motivate players beyond their capacities. Kelly inspired his team by using something called "pyramid power," whose mystical nature he'd become aware of after one of his children took a trip to Cairo. The team hired a U of T engineer to build a set of small pyramids, which he placed under the Leafs bench and, using astronomical measurements, pointed toward magnetic north. Over time the Leafs players also became convinced of their power. A larger pyramid—the size of a small camping tent—was made for the dressing room, which Lanny McDonald sat under before scoring four goals in one game. "After that," Tiger Williams said, "every guy on the team was fighting like hell to sit under it. Red convinced us that they worked and gave us some kind of advantage."

During dinner we sat with Red's wife, Andra. She was a lovely, beatific woman, a former figure skater who'd met Red while he was playing with Detroit. She told the story of how her roommate, Barbara Ann Scott, persuaded An to accompany her on a rendezvous with Gordie Howe, a meeting brokered by Scott's publicist. Gordie brought along Red for the same purpose, but cupid misfired and it was An and Red who fell in love. They courted for years before finally eloping in Moose Jaw. "I had to go on tour with my skating show," she said, "and Red had a hockey school to teach. So we had to do it then." If An's charm was any indication, I thought the old player/coach would have been an easy mark.

We found Red standing alone near the entrance to the hall. Over his shoulder, the lights of 42nd Street and Grand Central Station swam into view through the windows, the evening's quickening pace bringing the city to life. We introduced ourselves as the event's anthem singers—giggling at our own description—at which point Red's bright face bloomed brighter still. He thanked us for singing and shook our hands. We stood together and talked about hockey for forty minutes. Red did most of the talking. I asked him question after question after question about the 1974/75 Leafs, and what he remembered from that year. His details astonished. He described what had happened in each playoff game in the second round, his voice rising to a crescendo as he talked about the waning moments of game four, a 4–3 Leafs loss to Philadelphia.

"Salming had the puck in our end," he said, pointing to an imaginary spot halfway down the ballroom, which by now had emptied of most guests. "There was lots of time left, lots! But Salming, you know, he had this tendency. It was the tendency to slap the puck rather than wrist it. You see," he said, pointing to me and my wife, "you have way more control when you wrist it. Slapping the puck doesn't give you as much control, and that's what Salming always used to do. I tried to get him to stop, I really did. But he was stubborn. It's how he was, and when he had that puck, all I could think was 'Don't slap it! Don't slap it!' But what did he do? That's right, he slapped it. And of course MacLeish knocked the puck out of the air and scored to tie the game. Then we went to overtime, and we lost." The coach's arms fell to his sides. "We were a good team, a good team," he said, growing wan. "We really should have done a lot better."

Rapt, I'd been nodding along with the coach, but also waiting for a chance to ask about Keon. Then my wife asked a practical skating question, to which the coach shouted "Shack! This is how Shack did it!" He pantomimed moving in a wide stride across the marble floor, showing her where to place her weight and how to get the most out of the motion ("Skate like there's a barrel between your legs!" he said indelicately). It was a sweet moment: the Hall of Famer ordering my wife in her party dress to do as he did, arching his back just so under the low lights of the great building in the heart of Manhattan. Even in his dotage, Red Kelly could not resist coaching.

When An came to collect her husband, I realized it was my last chance to ask Red Kelly about Dave Keon. With An's hand at his elbow guiding him away, I coaxed them back. "Mr. Kelly, what about Dave Keon?"

Red looked at me. "What about him?"

"Well, what happened?"

Red's eyes grew dim. He made one hand into a fist and placed it in his other hand, grinding his knuckles into the open palm. The old coach shuffled a little.

"I don't know," he said, shaking his head.

A moment passed. For the first time that night, the coach said nothing.

Then, "I don't know ..." he repeated, each word parcelled out slowly. "I don't know where the angst comes from."

An tapped him on the elbow.

"Do you think he'll ever come back?" I asked him.

"I don't know," he said once more, sounding as if something in his heart had tightened. The old coach and his wife turned and walked out. We watched them cross the street, just to make sure they had.

7

The first Leafs game of the 1974/75 season came against a new team called the Kansas City Scouts. The only thing the boy knew about Kansas City was that it was a place in *The Wizard of Oz* and that a baseball team played there, too, a team that wasn't very good. It would be awful if the Leafs didn't beat the Scouts because they had no players the boy had ever heard of, although they did have a guy called Butch Deadmarsh, which the boy thought was a cool name. Still, if it wasn't bad enough having a collection of castoffs after what the boy learned was called an "expansion draft," the Scouts weren't even supposed to be called the Scouts, which was already pretty dumb. Instead they were supposed to be known as the "Mo-Hawks," which the Chicago Blackhawks vetoed. How "Mo-Hawks" ever got that far was amazing to the boy considering that, in Toronto, "mo" meant people who were gay, homosexual people (at his school, kids laughed at other kids whenever they said they were "mowing the lawn"). "Mo" was bad and no team called that could ever be any good. Even worse, they were scheduled to start the first two weeks of their hockey life playing on the road because the annual American Royal Rodeo and Livestock Show had been booked into Kansas City's Kemper Arena, forcing the Almost Mos to play second fiddle to a room full of cows and hogs. How anyone expected anything good of the team after that kind of beginning was hard to fathom.

The game ended 6–2, Leafs. Toronto played well, or at least as well as they had to play to beat a team as unfortunate as the Scouts, who would last only two years in the league. The boy and his sister had lain on their stomachs flat to the carpet in the TV room in the basement eating an enormous bag of plain-flavoured Hostess chips watching the Channel 8 broadcast, which started with some famous radio guy in a kilt and Scottish hat (called a "tam o' shanter") named Gordon Sinclair dropping the ceremonial first puck. Ron Ellis, Darryl Sittler, Ian Turnbull, and Jim McKenny scored the goals. McKenny had a rail-thin body with a massive afro that bounced side to side, and when the defenceman spoke— which he didn't do often—it was usually to say something funny. After the game, he told *The Globe and Mail*, "Right now [after one game], I do believe I'm leading Bobby Orr in the scoring race."

Even better than the Leafs winning, Keon scored on a breakout pass from Salming, and even better than that, it was his 350th goal of all time. After the puck went in, Ron Ellis used his stick to fish it out of the net before bringing it to the captain, who, without looking, held it at his shoulder for trainer Joe Sgro to take away. Sgro found some hockey tape which he stuck to the outside of the puck, writing "350" in black marker along the white band. Later, the camera zoomed in on Sgro holding the black disc before it panned to the captain sitting on the bench, his sideburns moist with sweat, his eyes riveted to the ice. To him, scoring his 350th goal was fine. But it was number 351 that he wanted more. You didn't have to be Dick Beddoes to see that.

The game would have been perfect had Keon been named first star, but they gave it to McKenny, with Salming and Inge Hammarström—who'd finished with three assists—getting the others. The next morning the boy made his way to school, excited about talking with Zirko and some of the others about Keon's goal and how Blaine Stoughton had skated head-first and unhelmeted into the goalpost ("After the game, the player had a king-sized headache," reported the *Globe*). So he was disappointed to find that, after a few days, people were mostly still talking about the fight between Roscoe and the boy-boobed Peters.

Peters's parents had been called to the school to meet with the principal. Roscoe's were called, too, but they never came, although the bully did return Peters's watch the same as he'd found it. The boy would grow up to be a man and learn—as the rest of society did—that it was just as important to talk to the bully as the victim in these instances, but in 1974 there was still the feeling that boys were just being boys whenever they fought, and that this sort of thing was part of a natural order that would, in time, sort itself out. The principal suggested that Peters dress more like the other kids in order to fit in. He also told him to simply walk away if it ever happened again. Roscoe was required to stay after school, where Mrs. Reynolds told him in a firm but gentle voice that in no way would punching or kicking other kids be tolerated. In the boy's mind, this only showed how cowardly the other teachers were, especially the men, who'd left it to the most generous and hopeful of them to sort things out. Besides, Roscoe would never listen to Mrs. Reynolds. Even if there were important things to learn from adults—like facts about God, the universe, and how machines worked, as well as why fighting was bad—you only had to look at Roscoe to know that trusting the opinion of others— especially the kind-hearted Mrs. Reynolds—was beyond him. Besides, instead of having been taught to listen and be polite and treat people with respect and not lie so that he could get into Heaven, Roscoe seemed to have been raised with a messed-up view of the world where you had to get the other guy before he got you and nothing anyone said was going to change him.

As the days marched on through science experiments with Mr. Motz and French with Mr. Guillaume and gym with Mr. Quirk, nobody engaged Roscoe in any kind of contact. In gym he'd sit in a corner by himself and throw rocks on the grass, while lunch saw him sitting alone at the end of a long table, swilling a can of Coke and forcing a white buttered sandwich with Kraft slices into his mouth before laying his head down on the table and sleeping.

One afternoon at the end of baseball practice—the boy had gone out for shortstop on the school's team, and had won the position—he left for home wearing his green and white Martingrove hockey jacket and carrying his Adidas bag. Walking across the school's common to the busy main street, he heard someone come up behind him, not close, but not far away. The person's steps were heavy, and when he thought of who it might be, he felt the entire weight of his soul lowered into the dark cache of his stomach, something he would only ever experience a few times in his life and always when something bad was about to happen. The sensation slowed his steps even though his heart told him that he should run, and run fast. A faint and distant screaming found his ears and his back became drenched in a terrible sweat.

"Martingrove?" said the voice behind him. "You guys suck."

The boy didn't know whether to turn around. He thought as he always did of Keon, how, no matter how nasty things became on the ice, he'd turn away and lean on his stick, focused on scoring the next goal as a way of making the other team regret what they'd done. The boy kept walking.

"Hey, homo, I mean you," said the voice, getting closer.

The boy turned around. "Hi."

Roscoe grabbed his arms and tripped him to the grass. The boy fell with a thud, his gym bag flying out of reach.

The boy lay on his stomach tasting the common, which was wet, loamy, and fresh like the insides of the earth. He knew better than to get up, even though it's what he wanted to do more than anything. He tried wriggling a little, but Roscoe lowered his weight on him. He sat on his back with his hand pressed against the boy's head.

"You like to eat grass, loser?"

"No."

"C'mon, it's good for you." He pressed the boy's face into the lawn.

"Did you see my fight the other day?" he asked the boy.

"Yes."

"Could you believe that faggot?"

The boy wasn't sure if this demanded an answer. He decided that it didn't.

"I like fighting," said Roscoe.

"K," said the boy.

"That's okay then?" said Roscoe. "Well, I'm glad I have your fucking approval, spaz," he added, smushing the boy's face a little more.

"The school says they don't want me to fight," Roscoe continued. "Well, not the school. It's that hosebag Reynolds. She's got it in for me. She doesn't have it in for you. You're her favourite, aren't you?"

The boy was going to say something about this not being true, although he knew it was.

"I hate browners like you. Always riding for free," he

said. "Makes me wanna puke. Although that guy Zirko, he's pretty funny. He's your friend, right?"

"Yes," said the boy through a mouthful of grass.

"You're lucky. It means I won't kill you."

The two boys sat in silence for a while, although Roscoe did most of the sitting—actually all of the sitting—while the boy lay stretched out like a beached porpoise. It was only after a moment that the boy realized that cars were passing and a few people were walking down the street, none of whom thought anything of the fact that one boy was sitting on top of another boy after school with no other kids around. To them, maybe it looked almost normal, like a game, which, after many years, the boy realized it might have been.

"You're the guy with all those Leafs pictures in his locker, right?" asked Roscoe. The boy told him that he was, even though lots of other kids had them too.

"Well, the Leafs are shit," he said. "The Flyers kicked their ass because the Leafs play like homos. The Flyers rule. Always have, always will. I like The Hammer most. He can beat up anyone whenever he wants. He beat the shit out of that queer Salming last year. Threw him around like a rag doll."

Were the boy having a normal conversation like the kind he would later have as a man with his friends, discussing teams and their stars and goons and the NHL, he would have pointed out that it wasn't Dave "The Hammer" Schultz—the Flyers' most feared thug and not only the worst person in hockey but probably the worst person in the world, too—who had blindsided and savaged a defenceless Börje Salming in last year's playoffs. It was Mel Bridgman, who had a thick moustache and a nose like a sunburned penis. The boy hated Bridgman for not fighting fair, but that was the Flyers' style, too. They fought dirty because they were too chicken to meet their enemies head-on. They fought in groups when you weren't looking. They fought when their victim was alone and most vulnerable.

The boy was appalled at how the Flyers cheated and bent the rules of the game in order to win, which they did a lot, winning the Cup in the previous season, 1973/74. A writer called them "The Broad Street Bullies," and pretty soon that's what everyone called them because that's what they were: bullies. They'd turned hockey into a crazy violent circus where their players would hit guys on the other team in a dirty way and challenge them to fight back, only when they did, a bunch of Flyers would jump in, forcing the other team to respond. When the dust settled the referees would give players on both teams penalties, but the Flyers would score because their best players, like Bill Barber and Reggie Leach, didn't fight. If the penalties went against them—which didn't happen often because even the refs (especially the refs) were intimidated by their team—the Flyers goaltender, Bernie Parent, who used to play for the Leafs, would stop most of the shots. Some afroed guy in the crowd behind the net in the Flyers rink—the Spectrum—would raise a hand-printed sign that said LAST LINE OF DEFENCE or IN BERNIE WE TRUST and before every game a fat lady in glasses and a dress would come out and sing "America the Beautiful," which the boy thought was wrong seeing as all the Flyers players were Canadian. Everyone in the Flyers crowd was large and hairy. Once, he'd said this aloud and his dad elbowed him in the ribs, adding, "And that's just the women!," a joke that the boy didn't really understand.

The boy liked fighting in hockey and bench-clearing brawls and it was exciting when players climbed into the crowd with their skates to get to the other team's fans, but the boy hated the Flyers because they looked like they lied and stole and didn't believe in God or Love or Heaven or had nice parents or would ever have been friendly to him if they'd met in public. They had cracked teeth and wild eyes and were slope-shouldered with snakes for hair. They looked like criminals, and that's what their way of playing hockey was like. After the boy became a man, he talked to ex-Leaf Jim Dorey, who confessed that he might have been partly responsible for the Flyers' style of hockey, which the boy as a man recognized as ironic. "I once had a fight with a Flyers player in my first year," Dorey told him, "and I beat him up bad. A fellow named Ronnie Ryan, who owned a TV station in Philly, told me later that the Flyers owner, Ed Snider, had a picture hanging in his office of me beating the crap out of his player to remind him that that sort of thing would never be allowed to happen again."

In the deciding game of the 73/74 series, the boy watched as Bobby Orr chased a puck down the end of the ice in the dying minutes of the third period only to be spun around and checked by the Flyers captain, Bobby Clarke, who had razors for teeth and a dead-doll look about his eyes. Clarke scored and Bobby Orr ended up on his knees, head down, staring at the ice in the mouth of the goal. It was the saddest thing the boy had ever seen: a great star beaten at the hands of such a godless group of players. The boy didn't especially like the Bruins—as a rule, he hated every team that wasn't the Leafs—but the pathos of the moment struck him, even though he wouldn't have called it "pathos," not knowing that word. In sports as in life, good guys were supposed to win; heroes were supposed to triumph; lawmen were supposed to put bad guys in jail; and someone—anyone—was supposed to stand up to the wretched bully. It's what the boy had read in every comic book and seen in every film, but the Flyers took that notion and gutted it, eating its flesh and leaving the bones to dry in the torpor of the sun.

Reaching for clemency and some middle ground, the boy said to Roscoe, "Well, Bobby Clarke played for Team Canada. In '72. Against the Russians."

"Yeah, and they fucking won it," he said.

"Four games to three," said the boy. For a moment their conversation had assumed an air of civility. They were actually talking about hockey.

"Still, the Leafs suck, don't they?" said Roscoe.

The boy lay there.

"Say it," said Roscoe. "Say it, spaz. Say it: Leafs suck."

The boy forced out the words.

"Okay, I'm fucking hungry," said Roscoe, reaching down at the boy's jacket and ripping the Martingrove crest—which was green and had a laughing beaver holding a hockey stick—from its stitching.

"Get up," said Roscoe.

The bully held the crest crumpled in his hand before throwing it at the boy. "Your team fucking sucks," he told him, "and you suck. And you're a fucking faggot for not fighting back," he told him. "What's your fucking problem anyway?"

The boy said nothing.

"WHAT'S YOUR FUCKING PROBLEM?"

Still nothing.

"We're gonna do this again, understand?"

"Yes," he said.

"Now fuck off, teacher's pet," he said. "Go home to your books and shit."

Roscoe turned and walked one way; the boy turned and walked the other. It wasn't until he was clear of the school that he burst into a storm cloud of tears.

8

For most of my life, my love for hockey has been inextinguishable. That I hated it for a handful of years—hated it for being the domain of the sheep-souled and the brick-headed, for being the single narrow thing that defined an entire country and its people—only made my love stronger and my thirst unquenchable. It was out of this love that I pursued the sport at full speed, and while I never equated my achievements in the game— or my intimacy with it—with those on the inside who'd survived its emotional and physical warfare, I felt like I knew a thing or two, and had done stuff that others maybe hadn't. In 2004, for instance, I travelled across Russia visiting hockey towns and meeting players for the purpose of making a documentary (*The Hockey Nomad Goes to Russia*). In the small industrial town of Barnaul I met up with the Russian National Team Legends, who were touring the country playing fundraising games against local teams. Before the game I asked if I might suit up and skate with the team—if only during warmup—and was told to get dressed. So there I was, pulling on long underwear and chewing my mouthguard alongside some of the greatest names to ever play in the Soviet Union: Yakushev, Anisin, Kapustin, Lutchenko, Kuzkin, and others. Once the game started they told me I could stay on the bench, but coach Bichokov threw me out for a shift, then another, then another, and by the third period I was on the starting defence pair. I didn't score, but I earned something better: the distinction of being the only Canadian to play with a Russian National team, their red and gold crest shimmering on my chest. If these kinds of adventures had given me reason to feel nearer the sport than I did from my living room, they also fed my delusion that I could somehow affect it. Which, of course, I couldn't, although for some reason the notion of drawing Dave Keon out of his exile to lead the suddenly curseless Toronto Maple Leafs to the Stanley Cup seemed, if not untenable, then not impossible. I told myself that this was my city, this was my life, and this was my team. I would find Keon and then, one day soon, they would win. Fans would be incited into a joyful, blessed riot that would stir the deepest slumber of the mightiest beasts in the farthest corners of the northern wild. We would howl at the crying sirens of victory and all that was wrong would be righted at last.

Still, if I knew anything about the sport, I should have known that even when you think you know everything, something happens to reveal the hubris of such a notion. When I got home from New York I discovered a detail so obvious about Dave Keon and the Leafs that I must have pushed it into the depths of my subconscious: unlearned it, kept it so far inside that it didn't infect my everyday life. This discovery produced a panic attack during a concert at the Air Canada Centre by my all-time favourite band, Rush. I'd been invited to the show by the band themselves. My friends were coming and it would be a great night.

Walking into the rink—which had long been hockey-less, the concert taking place during a labour dispute between players and owners—I settled into my seat with my giant arena beer and talked to someone in our group—a friend of a friend—who asked what I'd been working on lately. I told him that I had a basic concept for a new book—writing about looking for Keon as a way of coming to terms with my disaffection as a Leafs fan—and once the giant beer was consumed, and then another after that, we decided it would be a fine book indeed. I thanked the friend of a friend for his encouragement—it was the first time I'd told anyone about the idea—and then I looked to the top of the rink, where the banners of honoured players were strung across the rafters. I looked for Keon's name and number. My eyes went across the row, then back again, then back a second time. I repeated this once more, and as I did the lights of the arena dimmed. Within moments my favourite band took to the stage—playing "Subdivisions," no less—but still I strained through the darkness, looking for Keon's number. It wasn't there. I couldn't find it. Panic began to take hold.

My heart raced and I became flooded in sweat. I couldn't find Keon's number because it wasn't there. The realization that the greatest player in Maple Leaf history had no acknowledgment in his home team's rink left me dizzy-headed. All sense of mass or density left my body. I slumped at my chair like a man poisoned by drink or cross-bowed in the back. Head wedged between my knees, I wondered about the effect of the show's pinwheel lighting—I'd heard that sort of thing could happen—but even in post-song darkness I felt ill. Rush rolled through "The Big Money" into "The Analog Kid." I pulled my head from my lap and passed my eyes once more across the banners: KELLY, HORTON, GILMOUR, BARILKO. KENNEDY, ARMSTRONG, BOWER, SITTLER. SALMING. BRODA. I counted them. I read them aloud. There was no number fourteen. There was no Dave Keon.

I'd been given a special pass for the show to visit the band afterward. I wanted badly to go and see them. I also wanted to watch the rest of the concert since I hadn't seen much of it so far. At intermission, I collected my coat and told my friends that my kids were sick at home. I walked outside the rink. The cold air pushed into my lungs, feeding me oxygen. I hailed a cab and slid into the backseat, stilled in a kind of waking sleep the whole way home.

The next day the panic passed as I discovered that the absence of Keon's sweater was something that a lot of people already knew. One story had the team offering a sweater-raising ceremony as an olive branch to the retired centre, but Keon had refused, still bitter over past injustices and appalled that the team only honoured sweaters rather than retiring them. Another had the Leafs refusing to pursue the matter even after Keon showed signs of softening, although some believed that they hadn't even gone this far and had no intention of honouring the sour, ungrateful prick. Other people asked why the team couldn't have just staged a ceremony whether or not Keon attended. Either way, not citing the player had created an enormous vacuum in Leafs history. Years of team failure made his absence even more profound.

It was a few days after this discovery that I decided to go to old Maple Leaf Gardens, if only to effect a kind of balance after my dreadful experience at the new rink. Keon had played most of his career there, and besides, the building had reopened after years of sitting derelict while its owners—the Loblaws grocery chain—decided whether it made business sense to build another superstore in a dubious economic climate. In the end, they formed a partnership with Ryerson University, whose campus hub was close at hand and who committed to developing the building into an athletic centre replete with a refurbished ice surface.

That the project seemed suspiciously clear-headed and karmically alert—maintaining an ice surface would preserve the spirit of its old tenants—said as much about who was doing the planning as who wasn't. I thought the Leafs would have probably just fucked it up, turning it

into a Dollarama or a public-storage colossus, or maybe
a sweatshop or a wrought-iron internment camp like the
one in that dystopian movie starring Clive Owen. Just a
few months earlier, the building's doors had reopened to
the public. Friends described the retrofit as beautiful and
sensitive to the building's history, but I wanted to see for
myself.

Besides, I'd been invited there to play with one of my
men's teams, formed out of several departments of my
occasional employer, the *National Post*.

When I told friends where I'd be skating, they
corrected me, half-joking, "You mean the Mattamy
Athletic Centre, don't you?" They were only partly
right. When Ryerson first announced its intention to
rebuild the rink, the Leafs said they'd block any attempt
by the school to use the name "Maple Leaf Gardens,"
being unburdened, it seemed, of the time and attention
required to assemble a winning club. The Leafs claimed
they owned the name's copyright, another petty act from
an organization that stayed up late thinking of new ways
to empty the last few litres of karma from their nearly dry
supply. One thing the team couldn't prevent, however,
was the use of the building's old marquee, protected under
local heritage laws, which clearly spelled out the original
name of the rink, in blue serif no less, the grand letters
towering over Carlton Street. Below the marquee was a
set of glass doors—one of the first things the renovators
had done was liberate the small entranceways through
which millions of people had once squeezed—and it was

here that I first entered the restored building, my hockey bag wheeling behind me.

If I was cautious about how living with Keon's spectre would contribute to the pull of nostalgia—my last two books had been set in 1972, a trend that made me privately worry about becoming simply a chronicler of the past—it was all I could do not to throw up the flat of my hands to protect myself from the wave of memories that struck me as I entered the arena's concourse. The last time I'd been in the building I'd toured my newborn daughter through the abandoned concourse, just to say I had. Decades earlier I'd gone there as a child myself, holding my father's hand while moving into an arena swimming with bodies, strangers on strangers, a scrum of adult voices mumbling together. I could still smell them—aftershave, tobacco, Molson's—and I could hear them, too: the program vendors' gruff voices shouting one over another and the windowed ticket sellers, almost all of them female, authoritatively telling patrons what seats were available and what weren't for the game that night. The forces of the city gathered here at a time when Torontonians hardly ever came together, congregating once a year at the CNE or the Royal Winter Fair if at all (back then, there was no Toronto Film Festival or Nuit Blanche or Luminato or sparring music festivals to feed city life). Instead, the Gardens was Toronto's furnace and the fans were its coal. Once upon a time, it produced great hockey teams and great players. And none was as great as the captain, Dave Keon.

Archival photographs decorated the new/old rink, some the size of album covers, others printed floor to ceiling. Just beyond the entrance, the first print showed a crowd in 1967 cheering the Leafs' last Stanley Cup, an image meant to remind visitors how long it had been since the club was successful, or maybe how overdue they were. Another panel showed six faces in strip frames: Cyndi Lauper, James Brown, one of the blondes from Abba, Johnny Cash, Elvis, and Geddy Lee of Rush, all of whom had played the pale-bricked arena. There was also a large photo of a crowd sitting on fold-up chairs on the arena's temporary parquet watching a live performance of the Metropolitan Opera Company. I studied this photo as well as one of a crowd watching the Leafs in the 1940s. In each case the men wore suits; the women, shawls and dresses. Both crowds looked the same.

On the second floor were photos of different kinds of events: trapeze artists flung through the air as part of the Ramses Circus; a 1938 gathering of the Canadian Jewish League to denounce the persecution of Jews by Nazi Germany; a "Flood the Fund" night in support of Manitoban flood relief; George Chuvalo ducking under Muhammad Ali's flying jab; a six-day bicycle race around a makeshift Velodrome; ponytailed high jumper Debbie Brill vaulting over the bar at the *Toronto Telegram* indoor games; and the cherubic Jimmy Connors wearing a Leafs jersey and playing Ilie Năstase in an exhibition tennis match in 1980. Năstase, the villainous and tempestuous Romanian, was, naturally, dressed in Hab colours.

On the third floor was the motherlode of hockey photos: huge panels featuring Conn Smythe, Foster Hewitt, Ace Bailey, King Clancy, and scandalous owner Harold Ballard, the only one among them not smiling. There was Red Horner and a photo from the first all-star game with Howie Morenz. There was Syl Apps carrying the Stanley Cup wearing gloves like pot holders—the silver chalice svelte in its infancy—as well as shaggy-headed young people sitting outside the building on lawn chairs on a warm fall afternoon in 1972 waiting to buy standing-room tickets to see Canada–Russia, game two. On another wall: King George's funeral, portly Mackenzie King delivering a speech, and, on one broad panel, Pierre Trudeau wearing a long leather coat tied with a belt in the front, the young crowd converging upon him from the lip of the stage. Another image showed Bill Haley playing his fat-bodied white guitar on a small bandstand, while yet another showed the Harlem Globetrotters running around the court in tiny shorts with afros like broccoli florets. Another strip of photos framed Liberace; Elvis standing straight as a popsicle stick in gold lamé; Thom Yorke from Radiohead; Madonna moving about like a stoned moppet; Bob Marley, his eyes closed in the rapture of song; a caped Jimi Hendrix in 1969; Neil Young in suspenders and T-shirt performing "Trans" in 1986; and, sharp-eyed and grinning widely, The Beatles, who played Maple Leaf Gardens three times, the only place where they did that.

On the opposite wall was another set of panels running horizontally from top to bottom. Because game time was

approaching I headed for the dressing room, only to turn
back, deciding that I should see all the photos before
changing into my equipment. I noticed a small black-and-
white image featuring two players standing at centre ice.
One of the men had fair skin, small darting eyes, and a
square helmet shaped like a Kleenex box: St. Louis's Red
Berenson dressed in visitors' blue and red. The other man
had northern greaser hair, pupils as dark as tar, and fine
sideburns running perpendicular from his ear to his jaw.

Keon.

The photo was from New Year's Eve, 1971. Clarence
Campbell, the besuited league president, stood between
the players, about to drop the ceremonial puck. I was
thrilled to find Keon here, especially after his absence
at the Air Canada Centre. Whoever curated the photos
had understood the importance of including Keon in the
exhibit, knowing that fans like me would be warmed by his
photo, maybe even inspired by it. In Keon's image our very
lives were represented. It was important to have photos
of Ted Kennedy and Syl Apps hanging on the walls, too,
but those players, like their fans, had passed on. However
flat the soda of victory, Keon's generation was the last who
remembered. We were the surviving link to better times,
to winning times.

Before heading to the dressing room to play with the
other writers—we called our team the Finks—I wanted
to pay my respects to the player, feeling it was as close
to an intimate moment with my hero as I might get. I
walked over to where my hockey bag was sitting slumped

on the floor like a large, patient hound and grabbed my stick, which I'd balanced across the top of the bag. I brought the stick to the photo, and, looking over my shoulder to make sure no one was watching, passed the inside of my blade on the outside of the frame beside the captain's image. Farther down the hallway, a few late-arriving teammates came up the escalator. Taking one last look at the photo, I gathered my things and headed to the dressing room.

If studying Keon and returning to the roots of my love for the team had given me a certain perspective on the nature of time—or at least the tempo of its passing, first slow, then quicker with each year—I was careful not to write solely from the long view of a wise older person, remembering as a boy the tedium of adults who dwelled on their age or discussed everything that came after as against that which came before. Still, when it came to actually playing the game, age was a central part of my experience because most of the players on my teams were, well, old. Where younger players celebrated their ability to cut back and make three moves while travelling at great speeds on the edge of their blades, older players were thrilled to be moving at any speed at all. If sport, in general, was a celebration of life, playing hockey past forty was a triumph of getting off the couch midweek and driving to the rink then hauling one's bag onto a sop-floored dressing room before changing into old equipment and skating around a chilly oval trying to move only slightly slower than you had the week before.

These small victories would prove especially cogent in my first game in the new Gardens. After gathering on the bench and looking down the boards during the Zamboni's last few licks of the ice, it became obvious to me and the rest of the Finks that our opponents were nearly twenty years our junior. Besides their milk-and-honey skin and altogether robust behaviour—doing leg stretches at the bench that, from my perspective, evoked a sore memory of 1978—it was possible to handicap the team's age by the fact that many of them eschewed the use of shoulder pads or visors. They were of a vintage for whom skating around the ice open-windowed was another in a sequence of vain gestures, still young enough to feel cute or possibly handsome. Here the Finks had one advantage, for even though our youthfulness had gone out with Live Aid and the headband, we savoured every achievement, knowing it could be among our last. If our opponents were unaware of their athletic mortality—a condition the Finks felt compelled to reveal for them—we were more than happy in the bowl of the valley, having at least landed softly. For my part, I thought of Keon and his last season for the Leafs, an elder statesman among a new generation of kids: Sittler, McDonald, Salming. I tried to skate a little faster, shoot a little harder. I would will my way through the play as my all-time hero had.

The game took place under bright lights and the glorious, steel-ribbed original Gardens roof, the ice surface having been lifted from ground level to the new third floor. Once the game started, you could see that the young team—called DTRT, an initialism that was lost on me—were dangerous and vulnerable for the same reason. The nature of their attack came from the same place as their cageless helmets—more worried about how they looked than what they were doing. From the beginning, it was clear that garbage goals were beneath them and that they relied more on individual skill than team play, although at times they'd laser a puck off the crossbar or skate without contact through four players before running out of room. Still, every move seemed designed to impress a girlfriend who wasn't there, toe-dragging when they should have banked the puck off the boards, and skating wide into the corner to keep possession of the puck when a shot at the net would have at least resulted in a chance. After a while we could read the patterns ably enough to know what was coming, which, in sports, is often half the battle. While the young forwards sped about the ice, the Finks defence—among whose corps I patrolled—simply waited for the players to attack, knowing that the kids were loath to share the puck. Rush after rush, the DTRTs attempted a frivolous, if quick, move, only to see the puck swept from their sticks. We scored once, then a second time, then a third time. The DTRTs descended into checking us physically, but the referees were on top of things. Sticks were slammed to the ice, and pretty soon everyone who wasn't them was either a pussy or a faggot or a third word they couldn't find.

The game stood at 4–0 going in the last five minutes of the third period. It looked like we'd win, the young men having resigned themselves to the embarrassment of losing to a team of players as old as their fathers. Then, with the puck loose at the blue line, I took off toward centre ice. Intuitively, my defensive partner lifted it out of the zone. One DTRT reached for it, missed, then I cupped it on my stick before bursting down the ice, something I rarely did. As I crossed into the ocean of our opponents' zone there was a certain ah-fuck-it-ness about the rush, which is always the case with players like me who should know better. One of the chasing forwards could have checked me but instead he moved to my left, protecting a two-on-one developing as one of my teammates—the Finks' highest-scoring player—raced to get in on the rush.

Being a defenceman—pass-positive and always looking to head-man the puck—I had maybe one or two chances on goal every couple of games, so it felt strange being so close to the net with a clear view of the goalie. At first it hadn't dawned on me where I was and what I was about to do, but approaching the netminder's left, I realized that I had two clear choices: move the puck to my darting teammate or shoot the damned thing. I shot the damned thing.

The puck sailed into the top of the net, pushing out the netting like a breeze into a wind stocking. I hadn't scored this kind of goal in ages, maybe ever. I'd never roofed a puck before, and I'd never scored in a place as important to me as the Gardens. Rounding the boards with the dark pastry lying in the bottom of the net, I wasn't sure what to do next. As a tribute to Keon and the fact that the captain's unseen force may or may not have helped guide the puck through the air, or at least distracted the goalie in the form of a dancing blue spectre at the edge of his vision, I thought I should raise a single glove in the air before hiding it as if embarrassed for having done something I shouldn't have. Instead I whooped and grabbed my teammates, hugging everyone in sight.

9

After his encounter with Roscoe—he wouldn't have called it "bullying," since people didn't use that word back then—the boy came home drained of tears, plunking his gym bag on the landing at the bottom of the stairs. Moving quietly down the hallway to his room at the back of the house, he stopped in front of his bed before leaving his feet and landing BWOAFF in a starfish across his blue and white comforter, the softness of the bedding swallowing the hurt that consumed his body. The feet of the bed scraped across the floor and the round coils of the box springs wheezed like an old asthmatic man pushing a grocery cart. His mother called to him from the brightness of the kitchen: "So how was your day?" Feeding his words into the fat of his pillow, the boy said, "Fine. Good," although by the time they reached his mom they must have sounded like "feeghhhhooootttt." From the kitchen he could hear plates clanking in a cupboard and stove switches clicking on. Starving but exhausted and humiliated after what had happened—in the end he'd been no better than Peters, a useless punching bag for the scariest and toughest kid in school—the boy stretched out an arm and reached for his bedside table. He found his transistor radio and gathered it into his body.

The radio was round and silver, with two dials on the side and a small speaker grille on the front beneath a narrow windowpane with a red arrow that glided across the stations, both FM and AM. In the evening he'd secret the radio under his chin as if protecting a sacred bauble and set the volume to barely nothing while tuning in Maple Leafs broadcasts on CKFH. The quiet of the broadcast—the announcers' voices, the sound of the crowd, the faint rumour of action—made the boy feel as if he were listening to the game from a distance greater than Earth, maybe through one of those parabolic microphones he'd read about in *Scientific International* or *The Martian Chronicles*. At the same time, because the rest of the world was so quiet—his room, his house, his street, his city—the faintness of the sounds was somehow loud, and because he had to listen so hard, he heard things he wouldn't have heard at full volume: a fat popcorned fan in a peewee coach's jacket yelling at Dave Dunn on defence; Errol Thompson pushing out a gush of air—"DFFFTTT!"—after taking a floating puck to the stomach; the last trailing notes of the Gardens' organist ending a selection from *Fiddler on the Roof.* In these moments, silence grew loud and small sounds grew big. This made the boy feel big, too.

The boy flipped on his back, rolled the bauble on his stomach, and tuned the dial to his favourite station, 680 CFTR, hoping to lose himself in whatever was playing. Most other kids at school listened to the city's most popular station, CHUM—sometimes the boy did, too—but he liked CFTR more because it was newer, and because it was newer, it was better. Even though the boy would grow up to be a man who was distrustful of most new things, back then old and traditional and established meant something stale and dry and boring while new was bright and shining and fabulously charging into the glowing chasm of the future. New was something that was happening now and next and later, and since that's how the boy's brain and body worked, CFTR was a better station, even though it played more or less the same songs as CHUM, although one thing it did that the other station did not was play "The Streak" every hour at the top of the hour. "The Streak"—a comedy number by country joke singer Ray Stevens about people who took off their clothes and ran around in public, mostly at sporting events and award shows—was probably the boy's favourite song, which is not to say it was the song he'd remember most from his boyhood. Instead it was the songs that scared him and made him sad that he carried long into his life. They were also the ones he dreaded hearing, but listened to closer than others. Back then strong music was unsettling, like the effects of a strange potion or the first sign of a sudden terrifying storm. In a book the boy had once read about cowboys, an old codger smoking a corncob pipe had said, "Sometimes, you've just got to take your medicine and move on." The boy thought that maybe that's what listening to these songs was like.

He turned on the radio. CFTR was playing "I Shot the Sheriff," which the boy thought was a good song, even though, because he was only eleven, he couldn't really tell. In the song a deputy got killed, which the boy thought was cool because killing and death were cool, at least in this case, where a killer had been wrongfully accused. The story in the song could have come from a TV cop show— maybe *Mannix* or *Cannon* or *The Streets of San Francisco*—and the keyboards went *brap brap brap,* at least the boy thought they were keyboards. The song was by a guy from Britain named Eric Clapton and it came from an album called *461 Ocean Boulevard,* which the boy had been given by his cousins who lived in the basement of his uncle's house behind the backyard hedge. He'd found a picture of Eric Clapton in *Circus* magazine with long greasy seaweed hair wearing a purple shirt with a big collar, and he'd clipped it for his wall. He'd taped it up beside a poster of the Rolling Stones, and another one of Aerosmith. Beside that was Frank Mahovlich wearing the red and white of Detroit, and beside that was Davey Keon, his tongue curving around his lip as he reached out his stick trying to gather in the puck.

"I Shot the Sheriff" ended and a sad, terrifying song started, made even sadder and more terrifying considering what he'd just gone through. The song was called "Seasons in the Sun" by Terry Jacks, but the boy couldn't understand why it was called that because there was nothing happy or sunny about the song. While it was probably the first serious or "heavy" song he'd ever heard, it was also impossible to measure the true weight of darkness and fatality that absorbed him while it played, more so considering that, up until this point, most of the music he'd heard or the books he'd read or the movies he'd seen had been dusted with the icing sugar of fantasy. Death usually came in the form of lasers slicing open villains or bad guys thrown into volcanoes or flaming car wrecks shooting over a collapsing precipice. Like "I Shot the Sheriff" or "The Night Chicago Died" or Michael Murphey's horse ballad, "Wildfire," death was set to jumping drums and merry, excited pianos and stinging guitars. Death in most pop music was rarely mournful or funereal, a word the boy didn't know yet, but still.

The song started with a few guitar chords played with a wobbly sound, a sound the boy would later find out was called "tremolo," a word that made him think of a delicious flavour of ice cream not yet invented. The words went "Goodbye to you my trusted friend / We've known each other since we were nine or ten." The boy had listened to other music where the subjects of the song were also kids, but none of them had words like "Goodbye my friend / It's hard to die," which the "Seasons in the Sun" singer sang just as the drums kicked in. The song made the boy sad because the singer sounded sad. His voice was also a little like the boy's—young and mewling, weak-sounding—and because the subject of the song had a family, and because he was being taken away from them—the reason was probably death, although he couldn't be sure—the boy became vacuumed into the words, even though he resisted, something he always tried to do whenever CFTR played the song.

The boy felt his body settle into the loam of the bed, the mattress, sheets, and pillows making the world soft and forgiving through the desperation of the song, which continued: "Goodbye Papa, please pray for me / I was the black sheep of the family." The image of the black sheep terrified the boy—sheep were supposed to be white, but this one wasn't; that's how you could tell something was wrong, he thought—and there was another line: "Goodbye Papa, it's hard to die." It was the first time a song had ever talked about dying in this way, dying as something real and terrible and hard. It sounded as if the singer knew he was going to die, and this made the boy feel cold and sick. He'd seen this sort of thing a few times on TV, in cancer movies like *Brian's Song* or *Bang the Drum Slowly,* but it was never like this, never this bad. Nobody had ever seemed so helpless. Death had never seemed so inevitable.

In comic books, good guys overcame death. Ironman and Spider-Man and the Fantastic Four were forever descending to meet their fate only to be rescued by some last-minute miracle of power or twist of circumstance that would get them to the next issue. The same was true in hockey and the same was especially true of Dave Keon.

In 1974 the Leafs captain wasn't young. The boy knew this because Keon had won Stanley Cups back when he was just a kid chewing on his toy trains. The captain was thirty-four years old—only Norm Ullman and Eddie Shack were older—had scars around his eyes and mouth, and he used to twist his neck about when standing on the ice as if trying to loosen something that had tightened with the years. But despite playing through the rugged age of the Original Six and into what the boy would later learn was called "The Expansion Years," Dave Keon had kept going because, like Ironman and Spider-Man and the Fantastic Four, nothing could stop him. In the words of an old sportswriter whose column the boy liked to look at in *The Globe and Mail* newspaper—his name was Scott something and his son sang that popular "Heart of Gold" song which CFTR played a lot—Keon "roared against time while continuing to be one of the league's most dynamic and dependable forwards." The thought that death could come and get the boy's hero—or get the boy himself—had seemed preposterous until "Seasons in the Sun," which suggested that anything and everything was out there, even death, especially death. The third verse started: "Goodbye Michelle, my little one." The boy in the song was dying. The end was near.

But then something happened that always happened whenever the boy listened to the song. Just as he was about to force himself to turn off the radio and read one of his hockey magazines that lay on the carpet beside his bed (COULD CHICO BE THE MAN FOR THIS YEAR'S ISLES

RUN?), the song began to rise up, lifting itself through the sorrow and darkness. The singer sang higher and an orchestra played and girls who sounded like angels began oooohhhing in the background. The drums thumped and the guitar tremoloed and the singer repeated words about joy and fun and starfish. The boy wondered if Terry Jacks was trying to say that maybe death wasn't so bad, that maybe it all works out in the end. The boy didn't know, but there was lots he didn't know. Lots and lots and lots. "Seasons in the Sun" faded out—it sounded brightest and most positive as it was ending, the boy thought—and the next song was called "You're Having My Baby" by Paul Anka. He liked that one, too.

10

After playing at the Gardens, I thought I should talk to Jim McKenny, whom Leafs alumni called "Howie," and who was the first young defenceman of his era to be compared to—and cursed by—Bobby Orr. We'd exchanged emails over the years and had met on the street a few times. Jim was a friend of a friend, and he said he'd be happy to talk about Keon and the Leafs, whatever I wanted. Then, on a warm day in early November, my daughter reported, "This really funny crazy guy called on the phone for you. He kept saying, 'Your dad's gonna kill me! He's gonna kill me for sure!'" It turned out that McKenny wanted to golf one last time, which was fine. We rescheduled for a few weeks later, once winter had secured the skies with long grey clouds and hot chocolate temperatures.

During the interview, McKenny—who'd played for the Leafs through most of the 70s—proved to be a magnificent and compelling swearer, throwing "fucks" and "shits" about like pocket change, although rarely sounding aggrieved or angry.

More impressively, McKenny never stopped to measure whether his language was affecting me or anyone else sitting in the coffee shop. Nor did he care whether people were awestruck by how many times he could swear during a single thought, although I counted five "fucks" and three "shits" in one instance. Still, the player never used his invective as a sabre point or angry jabbing finger. Because he was warm and good-natured, if gloriously profane, I imagined McKenny as a father lying on a too-small bed on Hello Kitty pillows telling his child about how the Grinch was "a miserable piece of shit until that little green bastard grew a fuckin' heart," or something like that. To the ex-Leaf, "The Fuckin' Cat in the Fuckin' Hat" was the same story, as long as the creature wasn't found out.

I wondered whether McKenny swore as much as he did because he was making up for lost time not swearing during his days as a prolific television sportscaster. But while he spoke quickly and with great colour (mostly blue), the former player moved about slowly, and to shake his enormous hand was to fit one's fingers around those that had been gnarled after a lifetime fed into the grind of a contact sport. When burrowed tightly in thought, McKenny's weathered features suggested to strangers that they approach with caution, although a single burst of expression or gesture of mock outrage was enough to make his bright personality come alive like that of a friendly sleeping hound awakened by thunder.

McKenny had played infrequently with Keon during two call-ups in the late 60s, and more so in the early 70s until the captain's last season in 74/75. He remembered how, at first, "Keon yelled like fuck at me, screaming his head off trying to get me to do something the right fuckin' way on the ice. I was scared as hell and he was fuckin' hard on me, but it was fuckin' good. He was a good captain even though he was tough on me. But he had to be. I had no fuckin' idea what I was doing out there. No idea at all.

"It was the same with Sittler and McDonald, but especially Sittler, who was tougher than fuckin' nails. After a while he learned how to go to the net the way Keon did, who'd learned himself from guys like [George] Armstrong in the 60s. Sitting on the bench, you'd watch Keon and you'd see how he went from here to there to here," McKenny said, a crooked finger tracing the air. "Through Davey, you saw the ice as being more than just a place where a bunch of players were runnin' around. It's funny because I thought I knew the game, but I didn't know shit. Not compared to him. He was just so smart, so intense, and so fuckin' committed. He never missed a single shift, never stopped trying no matter how long he played. He was always out against the other teams' toughest guys, too, getting hacked by guys like Bobby Clarke and Bill Barber and shit. But the tougher it got, the tougher he got. The more intense the game, the more intense he was, and so on. You just couldn't keep him down because, no matter what, he was gonna keep coming at you. First time I saw that I couldn't fuckin' believe it. I thought, 'Holy shit, this is what the NHL's about. This is what it means to be a hockey player.'"

McKenny remembered the 74/75 Leafs team as a tight group filled with impossible and, to hear him describe them, ridiculous characters. Not even Ballard's rancour, and the problems he caused, could worry the team beyond the usual fears and anxieties of a pro athlete's life. McKenny himself was appalled by the Leafs owner. "I loved King Clancy, who was always at Ballard's side, but Ballard never paid him any money. Clancy's wife hated him for this, but he did whatever Harold asked. If he hadn't been around it would have been a fuckin' joke, but Clancy gave him credibility. Ballard was just a fuckin' loudmouth, a joke who couldn't run a team to save his life. The Leafs had no money back then, which is one of the reasons Keon and players like him had to get the fuck outta town."

I asked McKenny how the team reacted when Ballard would criticize their play. He waved a hand in the air and said, "Nah, it had no effect on us at all. Ballard talked all the time and said all kinds of stupid, misinformed shit, so it was no big deal to us. It was this constant fuckin' drone and we just ignored it, and I can tell you firsthand that one of the people it definitely did not fuckin' bother was fuckin' Davey Keon. Ballard said shitty things about Inge, too, which, let's face it, were just fuckin' untrue. Inge was tougher than fuck and strong as hell; same with Börje. One time, [enforcer] Kurt Walker was teaching Börje how to jab, and they decided to put on boxing gloves. Walk threw one punch and Börje hit him back, knocking him on his fuckin' ass. Tiger laughed so fucking hard I thought he was gonna lose it. But that's the way those Swedes were. They'd only just come to the NHL, but you couldn't knock 'em over on the ice. It was impossible. If Inge was playing today, he'd have scored ninety goals a season. No fuckin' question about that.

"In the beginning, the Swedes had to go through lots of shit," McKenny continued. "I remember one night after a brawl, we were sitting there on the bench, everyone just fuckin' bleeding everywhere. We were a sorry fuckin' mess. Timmy [Ecclestone; McKenny's roommate] turned to Inge and said, 'I bet this wasn't in the brochure, eh Inge?' We all laughed our asses off," he said, tipping back on his chair and howling. "I mean, the bench-clearing brawls were fuckin' insane. It was fine if you got out there early. You could grab a country-clubber, someone like Rick MacLeish. But if you ended up with Harvey Bennett, forget it. Harvey would get four bennies in him and he'd just go. It was fuckin' terrifying, and we had a tough team, too."

I asked McKenny about that year's West Coast road trip—the low point in the Leafs' season—and at first he struggled with the memory, telling me, "I was on speed all the time, so I don't have total recall. I'd just move on night after night. You could really drink on speed, too, which was great, and we partied all the time, although, thinking back, I can't even call it partying. It was just drinking. One beer and I was gone. But what the hell. I was flying all over North America with a pocketful of cash. Me and the boys didn't give a fuck for nothing. Nothing at all.

"Road trips, for me, were always one big fuckin' blur. I'd get the old lady to drop me off at the airport early so I could get in a five-hour shift of drinking before we left. All the fuckin' guys did. This would go on nonstop for six days. You'd do fine in Los Angeles, okay in Oakland, but by the time you got to Vancouver you'd fallen apart. We should have just mailed them the two fuckin' points and come home instead."

After finishing our coffees, I wondered how long it had been since McKenny had last seen Keon. "About six months ago," he said. "I was doing a thing for heart and stroke after my heart attack, and he was doing something for prostate cancer, 'cause he'd had that and come through it." I hadn't known about the captain's illness, so I asked McKenny if he was feeling better, and he said, "Fuck yeah. He looks fuckin' great." While this was a relief, it made me aware that if I wanted to find him and convince him to come home it would have to happen soon, because one never knew. I reached for the table and tapped it, then told McKenny what I'd been thinking: how the Leafs had to honour Keon before it was too late.

"Honour him?" asked McKenny. "What do you mean? How?"

"Well, with a banner," I suggested.

"There's no Keon banner at the ACC?" he said, surprised at the news.

"No," I said. "Everyone else is up there, but not Keon."

"No kidding," said McKenny. "Well, that's fucked."

"I want to try and bring them together," I told the defenceman. "The Leafs and their old captain."

"Naaaww, shit," said McKenny, passing an arm across the table. "If the Leafs asked him now—if *you* asked him now—Davey would just be embarrassed. He doesn't want to go through with all that," he continued, *pffffting*. "Most players hate all that shit. The whole focus is on something you did or didn't do fifty years ago. If it was a great organization it would be one thing, but the Leafs are so tarnished now. Who gives a fuck if a guy won four Stanley Cups fifty years ago? Besides, the Leafs have lost a whole generation of fans. Who knows if people would even care about him? The lack of the Leafs' success doesn't affect me emotionally. I don't give a shit. It does affect me financially. I mean, if the Leafs were doing well, I'd be doing personal appearances everywhere: at bars, rinks, shops. Billy Derlago says that it costs him twenty thousand in appearance fees because the Leafs are so shit."

For a moment the notion that people wouldn't care about Keon made me feel defeated, but because McKenny was a good guy, and because I'd grown wan after what he'd said, he told me, "From what I know, Davey has good days and bad ones. He's a stubborn Irishman, and although I don't think there was ever anyone in the history of this world who was more proud to be a Leaf, there's still lots of fuckin' bitterness there. But he seems better, at least when I've seen him. He seems good. Maybe he just spends too much time alone. Not many people see him. Believe me, if I fuckin' lived in Florida I wouldn't be racing to come up to fuckin' Bond Head for a golf tournament. But who knows? Maybe he'll talk to you. He's a lot better when he's around his brother, Jimmy. He's the guy you want to get to. If Jimmy introduces you to Davey, I bet he'd do it. In a heartbeat."

My heart leapt as I leaned in to hear McKenny's advice, the player's voice sounding a little tired by this point, perhaps wearied by the animated force of the conversation. "I mean, they don't go anywhere. They don't fuckin' go out. They live in West Palm Beach. Jimmy's going down there next month; at least that's what [former Canuck and Blackhawk GM] Dale Tallon told me. Just go down there," he said. "Keon'll do it. I mean, he has to."

I was buoyed by McKenny's estimation.

"After all," said the old defenceman, "you're not out to hammer anyone. I mean, you're not, are you?" he said, reaching with two hands for my neck.

11

For the rest of the week the boy was paralyzed with fear. He ran home faster than Bruce Jenner, and each time he was lucky to avoid Roscoe. During regular school hours the bully ignored the boy, looking through him even when he was looking at him. This worried the boy even more, not knowing what awaited him after school, or when.

Then, in the following week, Roscoe found him twice, taking the boy just beyond the doors, his rough hands on his shoulders pushing him to the earth. Mostly, Roscoe sat on the boy, slapped him in the head, punched him hard in the middle of his back, called him names, and then, after a while, left hungry for dinner. Sometimes the bully did worse things: sitting on the boy's chest and letting a thick string of gob drip until it reached the boy's face, landing warm and awful on his skin. In middle school, being gobbed on was one thing—it actually happened a lot—but having the bully's craggy face loom over his as the translucent oil of his insides fell on the boy was the ultimate schoolyard indignity. Whenever this happened, he wanted to fight back. He wanted to raise his arms and shock the bully with a punch. But he didn't and he couldn't. Many years after the boy became a man, he wondered why he hadn't told anyone what was happening—more so, he wondered why no one had tried to stop the beatings—but he was ashamed of what Roscoe had done to him, and besides, if word got out, he'd have been branded a spaz and a homo and a loser who couldn't stand up for himself. And if Dave Keon had resisted the temptation, so would he. The boy told himself that, somehow, all of this would play out evenly in whatever awaited him across the long shadow of the rest of his life. He let whatever happened, happen. He told himself that he had no choice.

In the hockey world, differing theories surrounded Keon's pacifism in the face of an intense and violent game. The boy would become a man who would meet Bruce Hood, the old referee, who, when asked why Keon never fought, said, "It just seemed to me that everyone liked him. At least that was my sense." Jim Dorey put it this way: "Players had respect for David because he'd never retaliate. And I mean, like, ever. He'd be going up ice getting slashed and pissed off, but he never turned around and gave it back. Instead, the next time the guy would be coming up he'd forecheck the shit out of him as a way of getting even. Lafleur was like that, and Gretzky, too."

In 1967—the year the Leafs last won the Cup—Dave Keon recorded but a single two-minute penalty. Stan Mikita, who played for the Blackhawks and was often shadowed by the Leaf centre, told the papers that he maintained a list of players with whom he wanted to get even, but that "I wouldn't think of starting with Keon. How could I? He keeps his nose clean and he's simply too nice for me." Coach and broadcaster Harry Neale also said, "No matter how violent the game got, goons, for some reason, stayed away from Dave Keon." The boy thought it was impossible to respect and admire the player any more than he already did—the boy didn't use the word "love" to describe his affection; that would have been weird and gross and just wrong—but the fact that he was the league's nicest player was almost too much. In general, the boy was drawn to things that were nice as opposed to bad, things that were gallant as opposed to cowardly, things that worked in the name of good rather than in the name of evil. The greatest things were nice— his mom, his teacher, his favourite team, his room, his street, and God and Love and Heaven—while the worst things were bad—Roscoe, the Flyers, lying, cheating, stealing, fighting, and Hell. He told himself this while walking home after his beatings. He repeated the list of good things versus bad things over and over, and even though he sometimes heard a voice raspberrying at him from a dark corner in his thoughts, calling him a loser and a chicken for not doing anything, repeating the list was good because at least he wasn't thinking of how his head throbbed or back hurt or how he could only hide his torn and savaged coat for so long.

Weekends were a reprieve, and on Saturday nights the boy and his family would go to his aunt and uncle's house to watch the Leafs play, even though the only ones who'd watch the game would be the boy and maybe his dad, although his dad would also spend time visiting with the other adults, who weren't hockey fans. The boy would watch the game no matter what because watching and cheering for the Leafs was the most important thing he could imagine doing. It was his job and his duty and part of his devotion as a fan, and he took it seriously, as seriously as anything in his life. If there was a Leaf playing in "Showdown"—an intermission feature where players took penalty shots and did skill challenges wearing pinnies on a small rink somewhere in suburban Toronto—that player had to win. If the all-star team was announced and a Leafs player wasn't on it, it was the result of gross injustice, and magazines that didn't have anything in them about the Leafs weren't worth reading. A radio or TV program about hockey that didn't mention the team was a lousy program with stupid announcers and, absent Toronto players, the gum in a hockey card pack tasted bitter. The boy felt that if he didn't stand up for the Leafs, something about his life and the world and the order of the universe wouldn't be right, and while he would become a man who would sometimes look back on this slavish commitment and shake his head, he also knew that it made him feel important at an age when everything about his young life seemed insignificant. Besides, the Leafs were playing Buffalo, and while Buffalo were good, the boy thought the Leafs could probably beat them, although back in those days, the boy thought the Leafs could probably beat anyone at any time, which was the opposite of how he would feel as a man.

A few hours before game time, the boy and his sister scissored their way to their aunt and uncle's house through the hedge at the back of their yard. The boy was eleven and it was one of the few things his parents let him do alone, although it's not as if the boy needed to feel independent. In fact, independence and responsibility terrified him and the time away from his mom and dad but especially his mom made him feel like one of those small robots in *Silent Running* that gets shot into the horrible floating vastness of the universe out of their tiny lonely spaceship. The boy liked his tether, but he could handle moving through the hedge on his own. Even though he'd grow up to be a man who would travel the world and live to wander strange roads in new cities, the boy would always remember those first few moments in the moist uncertainty of the bushes behind the house and the shadows that darkened his first steps inside. Lost for a moment in the leafy folds of the hedge—the top of the bushes rising above his height—he let himself disappear from view only because he knew that, on the other side, his mom would be waiting there, partly because she didn't want him to feel frightened or uncertain and partly because, like all parents, there was a grim place preserved in her imagination where her children didn't get through to the other side. But after a few trips she stopped greeting them, and on those subsequent occasions, when the boy or his sister suddenly appeared a little older, a little taller, a little more mature, she, like all parents, felt a pinch of regret, knowing that those trips across the hedge would eventually build to a road down which they would keep walking.

Coming out the other side, the boy found his uncle standing at the barbecue beside the garage. It was early November, but still the glow of autumn held, the evenings carrying a suggestion of warmth, if not warmth itself. His uncle—a mechanic who wore an undershirt and black trousers no matter the year or season or style of the times—poked and flipped square hunks of meat on the open grill, smoke clouding his face, which was further clouded by a cigarette hanging gold-banded at its smouldering tip. His uncle shouted, "Ey Bish-kwee!" after seeing the boy and his sister come through the hedge. "Bish-kwee" is what his uncle had always called him—a corruption of the boy's last name—and while nicknames bothered him, this one didn't because of the way his uncle said it, barking like a lion-tamer before a great trick or an emcee introducing a singer, eyes bright and arms thrown open, which, in this case, held a pair of glinting tongs drooling grease in the late-day sun.

The two families ate at an enormous table in the living room pressed close together to create a jangling symphony of knives and forks darting from platter to plate to mouth. Eating was a loud and joyful scrum. The atmosphere was freer and brighter than at home because the adults were busy talking to each other, and because they were, the boy could get away with stuff. If the boy's home was a fortress of rules and his days locked into a schedule imposed by school and homework, his aunt and uncle demanded nothing of him other than drinking as much pop and eating as many sweets or bags of chips as he could. Sometimes during the week the boy's uncle was at home in the daytime, a strange thing for an adult to do, but because he owned his own garage his hours were flexible. On lost July days the boy would pass through the hedge to find his uncle drinking a few beers strung together by plastic netting held by bare arms slick with sweat after hours of engine work on an iron colossus dragged home to his garage from the shop. The boy would sit and talk with him and his uncle would offer him a beer, then wink at him. His aunt winked a lot, too, passing him chocolate before meals and pop after breakfast, and although the boy's aunt was his mother's sister, there was something different about them: one older, more formal, more studied, more 1950s; the other wilder and more outrageous, smoking and drinking and swaying with the casual glory of the times, a 70s totem in macraméd top and gold jewellery. Weekend dinner pressed these forces together, and with the boy's uncle conducting the meal while passing around one enormous platter of food after another, it seemed like the perfect pregame routine: a lively and resplendent feast before the boy settled on the tribune to gaze over the evening's match.

The boy had two older teenage cousins, Terry and Stephanie. For most of his young life he'd been welcomed into their rooms, which were in the basement down the hallway from the rec room, which is where the boy watched the Leafs. Even though Terry's door had a KEEP OUT! sign with a skull wearing an army helmet and smoking a cigar, he was often waved inside. Terry had a small bed and a desk of his own with an orange lava lamp that the boy, as a toddler, used to stare at for minutes on end. Beside his bed were stacks of magazines—*Popular Mechanics, Argosy, Equinox, True Stories, Mad, Cracked*—which the boy read lying on the floor while his cousin made sci-fi pencil drawings at his desk, holding up the pages to get the boy's opinion, which made him feel special, too. He wanted to know: Should the bad guy with the two cyborg eyes have a horn that shot lasers or searing liquid chemicals? Should Captain Conquest's ship have an anti-gravity shield or would it be more useful if it were amphibious? They'd talk these things out before the boy's cousin decided what to do, and eventually his other cousin, Stephanie, would come in and ask what was going on, even though the same thing was going on every time. Wearing cut-off jean shorts and a pink tube top in both winter and summer, she'd kneel in front of Terry's milk crate of records, fingertip them with rainbow-painted nails, and pull out that one with the scruffy men peeing against the wall or the naked blond children climbing on their stomachs up the mountainside or the purple cover with the melting heads. The boy thought that rock music— the kind of music his cousins liked—was a little strange and loud and probably too serious for him, but after his cousin showed him a record called *Electric Ladyland* by a band called Jimi Hendrix, he realized that he didn't know anything at all. The record had about a dozen naked ladies on it, kneeling and reclining, their boobs hanging out. This made the boy feel dumber than ever when it came to understanding the adult world, but he was also beguiled and engrossed by the images, two words the boy didn't know either. His cousin would play the record and tell him to listen for a single guitar note in a song called "Voodoo Child," which his cousin said possessed "the greatest note played in the history of rock music."

"Hear it? Hear it? There!" he'd shout.

The boy said he'd heard it, but he hadn't really. Like a lot of strange and interesting things, it had gone by too fast.

That night, the Leafs ended up losing to the Sabres. The score was 6–3. The boy didn't like any team who weren't the Leafs, but he didn't hate Buffalo like he hated some teams, even though the Sabres had been in the league only a few years and were already a little bit better than Toronto. Buffalo had a line called "The French Connection," named after a movie his parents had seen at the Westway Cinemas. *The French Connection* (the movie) was supposed to be pretty violent—the *Star* and *Globe* had said this—but "The French Connection" (the hockey line) were not. Unlike Dave Keon—who was Irish Canadian and who came from a French town close to Ontario—the members of the Buffalo line were all French from Quebec, although their right winger, Richard Martin, had a name like one of the boy's classmates. The French Connection were fast and scored like crazy. Their centreman, Gilbert Perrault, was nearly toothless with a wide crinkled face like Popeye, and he skated in great loops that made the other team dizzy the way the boy had once become dizzy after riding one of those spinning rides at the Ex. The other member of the French Connection was René Robert, which Zirko said was a gaylord's name, but the boy knew that some French guys, like some Italian guys, had girls' names, and that's just the way it was in weird places like Europe and Quebec.

The French Connection didn't need to fight, so instead they let their teammates do it, players like Jerry "King Kong" Korab, whom the boy hated, but also sort of feared. But it wasn't the fighting Sabres that the boy disliked most. It was the other players, like Don Luce, who had stupid hair and a weird thin face, or Craig Ramsay, who had a dumb helmet, or Morris Titanic, who had a stupid-sounding name (both first and last), or Rick Dudley, who wore a headband and tripped people, then tried to make out like he hadn't. Lee Fogolin also had a stupid-sounding name, and even though Jim Schoenfeld would end up becoming one of the boy's favourite players after the boy grew into a man, you had to admit that "Schoenfeld" was a pretty dumb name, too. As opposed to Keon. Which was short, sharp, and perfect. Like the man and the player himself.

The boy was disappointed that the Leafs had lost. After the boy became a man, he would learn—or attempt to learn—the technique by which he could "shake things off" or "take things one game at a time," but at eleven years old this was impossible (although, truthfully, it wouldn't get any easier). He shuffled to the basement stairs and thought he should probably go up and see his parents and maybe go home. Hearing loud talking and the clinking of glasses above him—his sister had fallen asleep in her aunt and uncle's bed—the boy turned around and walked to Terry's room. Standing outside, he put his hand on the door marked KEEP OUT!

It felt hot.

By 1974 his cousins had grown into older teenagers, eighteen, not sixteen and seventeen, not fifteen, respectively. Their hair had grown and they no longer moved with the quick snap of adolescence. Suddenly there were no more sci-fi drawing sessions, no easy efforts to humour or engage the boy. Instead, his cousins now affected the dark glow of young adulthood, although it wasn't so much their appearance as a new, mature scent, in this case, a strange kind of smoke like sweet flowers set on fire that seeped under Terry's door frame, a warm, wet perfume licking the wood panelling.

After a moment the door opened and his girl cousin, Stephanie, danced out and nearly fell over the boy. "Whhhoooheyyy!" she said, her face exploding with surprise. "What's going on, little cousin?" she asked in a high voice, her eyes bright, watery, and red.

"Nothing. Leafs lost," he said.

"Oh, man, that's a drag and a bummer," she said, patting his head. He hated it when people patted his head.

"Go in, go," she said, waving him through the door. "We're just hanging out, listening to tunes. Go in, little cuz."

The burning sweet flower smell was strong inside and there was a mist in the room, too: grey, hanging in the air. Terry was lounging on his bed while Samson, Terry and Stephanie's neighbour, sat at the desk. Samson had the look of a finely preened wolf. He wore tight jeans and a denim vest with no shirt as well as brown leather shoes with enormous black heels and white piping. A gold medallion hung on his chest in the shape of a leaf or peace sign or musical note—maybe it was all three, thought the boy—and it bounced a little as Samson turned around to greet the visitor: "Who calleth forward the cherub!!?" he shouted. "To what do we owe this divine appearance, oh small corporal of our suburban glen?"

The boy never understood anything Sam said, and it bugged him, as if his cousins' friend was somehow making fun of him, talking in a language he couldn't understand.

"How'd the boys do?" asked Terry.

"The boys?" asked the boy.

"The Leafs? Did they win?"

"Or did they blow it again?" asked Sam. Sam was a Bruins fan.

"Well, they didn't blow it," said the boy, defending his team, which is something he did all the time, seeing as it was his job and duty as a fan. "But they lost. 6–3. To the Sabres."

"Bummer. Now, excuse me, Billy Barty, while I tend to my previously heretofore machinations," said Sam, turning his back to the desk.

"How'd Keon do?" asked Terry, propping up a pillow on the bed.

"I think he got an assist. He played really well, though," said the boy, even though he wasn't sure that he had.

"Oh well. He's still the Leafs' leader," said Terry.

The boy thought it was a silly thing to say—obviously Keon was their leader—but his cousin was just trying to be nice.

"Like what we've done with the place?" asked Terry, gesturing at the walls of the room, which, the boy noticed, had been layered with posters he hadn't seen before. Instead of Terry's *Zardoz* photo and his Toronto Argonauts calendar there was a large cartoon of three fat men with crazy weird eyes smoking huge cigarettes—the Freak Brothers—and beside that was a poster of a smiling girl wearing a mesh T-shirt that showed her boobs and sharp darting nipples that made the boy wonder if that's what all girls' nipples looked like. Next to that was a psychotic-looking man with dripping black eyeliner wearing a top hat and holding a snake with gothic writing underneath that said WELCOME TO MY NIGHTMARE. Next to that was The Beatles from *Let It Be* and next to that was a guy with his hair swept high on his head, a sneer creasing his creviced face as he pointed a huge gun at the camera,

GO AHEAD, MAKE MY DAY written in big block letters under it. But the biggest poster of all had a small cartoon girl with big eyes sniffing a flower. The paper was knitted in what looked like yellow and blue foam, raised on the page. Out of the flower came bubbles that had gone into the girl's nose, and it looked like the girl was maybe sick, or certainly affected in a peculiar way. That the girl was smiling meant that she felt good, something the boy didn't understand. The last time he felt affected he'd thrown up, which wasn't fun at all.

The thing the boy noticed most in the room was that Terry's Dave Keon 1971 hockey card was missing. It used to be pasted above his cousin's headboard, but someone had taken it down. In its place was a face painted in wild swirling colours and a long finger pointing out: TIMOTHY LEARY WANTS YOU TO TURN ON!

"Where's your Keon card?" asked the boy, sounding as outraged as his small voice could produce.

"Oh, you know," said Terry, "just thought I'd change it up a little."

Sam turned around on his chair.

"Keon's over the hill, lollypop. He's an old man. Change and decay, parson, change and decay," he said.

The boy detested Sam for lots of reasons, and one of those reasons was how he walked around like he was the greatest thing going, how he thought he knew everything. The boy would grow up to become a man who could easily identify someone who was trying too hard to prove he was something other than who he was, but as an eleven-year-old it was more of a sensation, a hunch, a taste in the air that made him feel as if Sam was acting when he didn't have to be. Even worse, the boy's cousin Stephanie admired Sam for this quality. She was always tweeing and mooning over him, something the boy couldn't understand. And sometimes, when the boy, being small and unnoticeable, came upon Sam touching Stephanie on the couch or lying next to her on a lounge in the backyard, it made him even angrier that Sam was the way he was, that the adult world allowed him to do what he did. And now he was badmouthing Keon, which made him think of Roscoe, his brain and heart and stomach twisting at the thought of the bully.

"Besides, the guy hasn't scored bupkus this year," said Sam. "Not that I care, really. Like I told you, bro," he said, pointing at Terry, "the Leafs blow chunks and they won't ever win another Stanley Cup."

"Just get back to work," said Terry, which, to the boy, seemed like a weak response that deserved better.

"Keon is still the captain of the team," said the boy, mounting a pea-shooter's defence.

"And Brezhnev is still the King of Russia, little man," said Sam. The boy hated being called "little man" even worse than he hated having his head patted.

The boy imagined how Keon would respond to Sam before realizing that Keon wouldn't do anything because Keon didn't fight. Instead, he thought about the Leafs' new player—the rookie with a face like dented gypboard whose name was Tiger Williams—and what *he* would do if Sam had talked to him that way. Tiger could fight, and he could fight fast, his hands moving as quick as lightning at his opponent. Before training camp he'd told a reporter: "I'll make this team because I want to play hockey more than I want to eat." He also told Rex MacLeod in the *Star:* "I like to get in there quick with my punches, and, you know, surprise the other guy." Tiger's fists were as square as bricks and he had that vengeful cowboy look about him, like someone who'd been cheated down the road and was about to exact revenge, making right what was wrong. The boy imagined Tiger walking over to where Sam was sitting and smashing his face into the edge of the table, fountains of blood spurting everywhere. Tiger pounded and pounded him until Sam's face turned the colour of an old pear smushed in the back of the fruit drawer, and then, after Sam had begged for mercy, he put two fingers up his nose, pulled him to his feet, and landed a final, blinding shot.

"Here, cuz," said Terry, reaching into the night table beside his bed. "You can have it," he told him, handing the boy the Keon card. As the boy studied it, the captain's face grew large, then small, then large again, and for the first time the boy noticed small details in the player's appearance: the dented chin, the caterpillar scar that ran across his left eyebrow, the dark stain near his right temple. The captain was smiling, too, and you could see his missing teeth. The boy held the photo as if it were made from ancient parchment, treasuring the possession the way all kids treasure anything that's ever given to them as a gift.

"Okay, light show!!" shouted Sam, leaping from his chair and turning off the switch on the wall. Suddenly the room grew dark except for the weird poster of the swollen-eyed girl, which glowed in the black light.

"Dig this, cuz, dig this!" said Terry excitedly.

The room pulsed with a blue-purple glow. Sam moved to the stereo where he put on a song by Slade called "Mama Weer All Crazee Now," in which the singer started by howling like a wolf. The room began to swim and the boy asked himself why the ugly howling men wanted their mothers to think they were crazy, and why were they proud of it anyway? The first line of the song was "I don't want to drink my whiskey like you do," which made the boy think the singer was alcoholic and obviously a very bad person, but again: why would he put that kind of stuff in a song? With these questions racing into his head, the boy thought he might pass out. He clutched the hockey card, trying not to crease it. Stephanie stumbled into the room and shouted over the music: "You didn't, not with David here, did you??"

"Relax," said Terry.

Sam went back to the desk, stuffed a few things into his pocket, then stood up. His gold medallion flickered against the light and the white piping on his platform shoes glowed. He started to dance, his hips thrusting out, his arms raised over his head. His wild blond hair swung to the thumping of the drums and he kicked out his legs whenever the guitar played its main riff, which went *chug-a-chug-a-chug-a* over and over. Stephanie mooned at him from the bed, pressing her hands together in thrall. Terry closed his eyes and pumped his fists to the beat of the song. The music looked like it was driving Sam crazy as he thrust his hips harder and harder and waved his hands at an even greater velocity. The boy felt terrified because he feared that what the song was saying and what Sam was doing and the fact that his cousin had taken down Keon meant that the world was changing and nothing would ever stay the same. It was the late evening, but his cousins were acting as if it were the middle of the day, which made the boy realize that life existed after dark, and that people did things like this when he was asleep, lost in a dream while others shouted and danced and acted crazy. In that adult-lit moment, he felt caught in a place governed by neither time nor reason, but, more than that, he didn't feel entirely like a boy, at least not in the usual way. Suddenly everything was different. Well, maybe not everything. He looked down at his card and reminded himself:

Keon was still a Maple Leaf.

He was the captain.

12

If the early to mid-1970s Leafs were my favourite vintage—crack-toothed, helmetless, wild-haired, and Keoned—their charm and character was occasionally matched by the free-spirited and irrepressible—if defensively immature—John Brophy teams of the 1980s, as well as the 92/93/94-era Pat Burns clubs, which I wrote about in my second book, *Tropic of Hockey*. While the Mats Sundin–captained teams of the early to mid-2000s were almost as successful as their 90s cousins, I've always harboured a certain amount of guilt for not having fallen as hard for them. I felt somehow distanced by Sundin's calm and graceful yet emotionally reserved comportment, while I kept at arm's length the team's supporting cast of Gary Roberts, Alexander Mogilny, and Alyn McCauley. This was partly because a lot of the club's success was based on post-season domination of the pallid

Ottawa Senators, and partly because winning decisive games against middling teams like Buffalo and Carolina was always beyond their reach, Sundin's leadership falling short by degrees in the same way that his career never quite ascended to a galácticos height. Besides, the tall centreman had originally been acquired from Quebec for my second favourite Maple Leaf, Wendel Clark. Looking back, winning my heart after supplanting the player whose number I wore in rec hockey would have been impossible had Sundin not delivered a Stanley Cup to Toronto. Which he never did, ultimately saving his best hockey for Team Sweden in the 2006 Turin Olympics.

Another reason I couldn't establish any depth of relationship with Sundin's pre- and post-twenty-first-century Leafs was that first-time parenthood had resigned me to following the team with eyes half-shuttered and a body willing itself to stay awake till game's end. That, and the fatigue of losing, seemed to catch up to me. In the end, Sundin's Leafs of 2002–2006 were just another chimera, another siren, another ghost leading devoted bluebloods like me down a blind alley with a hill of rubble at the end.

While the Leafs of the 1980s weren't any more successful than Sundin's, at least they were young and guileless and haphazard, losing as spectacularly as they won. The forces that supported the relative gifts of players like Russ Courtnall and Wendel Clark and Al Iafrate and Gary Leeman were mostly fumes of enthusiasm and a general sense of where the other team's net was. The 80s Leafs—nicknamed "The Hounds" because of a few players' connection to Notre Dame College in Wilcox, Saskatchewan—had little regard for the subtleties of the left-wing lock or defensive-zone play (or any other zone play, for that matter), producing scores like 7–5, 8–4, 6–3, and 10–6, sometimes in their favour, but often not.

The 80s Leafs were also the opposite of emotionally reserved. This was largely owing to their coach: John Brophy of Antigonish, Nova Scotia. One of the original templates for George Roy Hill's movie *Slap Shot,* Brophy had been a career minor leaguer whose legend followed him around. His Maritime disposition was like that of a steam kettle forever on the verge of boil: a man who moved about life with his hands curled into fists. There were rumours—later confirmed by Jeff Jackson—that the coach kept a heavy bag in the dressing room of the Leafs' farm team in St. Catharines, which he whaled on between periods. Brophy was, in his own way, a brilliant motivator— players loved playing for him—and just crazy enough to commit to a lifetime of studying the game despite stops in countless backwater minor league towns before finally getting his chance with the Leafs, the only NHL team he'd ever coach. After leaving Toronto he kicked around the minors for a decade more; despite retiring for a few years, he came back in his early seventies and the legend continued to grow. Once, during a road game, he poured hot coffee on fans who'd been giving him a hard time behind the bench, scalding their hands and faces. After the game the police came looking for the old coach—this had happened before, so the players knew the drill—but the team had already zipped him up in an equipment bag, which they carried over their shoulders out of the room and into a bay of the team bus. They drove for twenty minutes before stopping to retrieve their coach.

I loved Brophy because he was unfiltered, and it was this unfettered approach to the game that gave way to the play of Wendel Clark, who, in another coach's hands, might have been restrained from throwing his body about the ice and establishing himself as one of the greatest bodycheckers, best fighters, most prolific clutch-goal scorers, and highly valued wingers of his time, outlasting the other Hounds to lead the '93 Leafs to their greatest playoff run since the late 70s.

Still, you could take all of these players and pour their statistical achievements and heart-shuddering moments into a tank and they still wouldn't rise to the level of what Dave Keon accomplished as a Maple Leaf. Nineties captain (and Hall of Fame inductee) Doug Gilmour was a fierce, compelling leader—small-framed like Keon, too—but he played only parts of three seasons in Toronto. Clark's tenure was just slightly longer—although nearly as mythic as Keon's—and Mats Sundin never settled into the raw matter of Leafs fandom. The closest any player came to matching Keon's achievements and hold on the city was 70s centre Darryl Sittler, who assumed the captaincy after Keon left. But Sittler's eventual parting from the team was played out through press warfare between the skater and an aging, demented Harold Ballard, who traded Sittler to the team that had ravaged his playoff dreams: the Flyers. In the end, Keon retired with four Stanley Cups; Sittler retired with none. Like Sundin, his greatest game might have been played under international auspices, scoring the thrilling Canada Cup–winning goal against Vladimir Dzurilla and the Czech national team in the fall of 1976.

I'd met these players before, and I liked them all. Sittler had fetched my tuxedo from the Leafs office before I first sang the anthem at Maple Leaf Gardens— "Good luck out there," he'd told me, handing over the rack—and the first time I encountered Wendel was at Baba's Lounge in Charlottetown, my words trapped in my throat as I told him, "I'm the guy who wrote that song about you ['The Ballad of Wendel Clark']." He replied, "I know. I've got a copy of your album up on my wall." The rest of the evening was played out drinking and jamming with him, P.J. Stock, Lanny McDonald, and Bryan Trottier, which amounted to pretty much the greatest few hours of my life.

One of the reasons I wanted to meet Dave Keon was to find out if the qualities I'd projected upon him were true, or whether it had all been a watercolour memory of childhood. In this regard, I'd resisted feeling cynical for as long as I could. Aging didn't help because aging fed cynicism and bitterness like coal to a hearth, and even though my life was good and I'd been lucky enough to do what I loved to do—"Don't get me wrong, I'm happy to be doing what I'm doing," I'd tell people after complaining about something or someone, which I did often—

there were times when I went looking for the smoke of dissatisfaction, purposefully darkening my view.

I was conscious of not being too romantic about Keon and the Leafs' past—romanticism would age me even quicker than cynicism, I warned myself—but while researching the life of the captain, I found that this admiration was largely justified. I discovered new things, for instance, that confirmed the captain's character and identified him as someone who was loyal to his teammates and who used his standing in the community to do what hockey players once did.

In 1987 Keon testified for ex-Leaf and Sabre Brian "Spinner" Spencer at his murder trial in Florida. Spencer had idolized Keon during his time playing with the Leafs, having grown up in Fort St. James, B.C., watching games broadcast from Toronto on a small black-and-white set.

Spencer's start with the Leafs had been fraught with drama. On December 12, 1970, his father, Roy, drove to CKPG television in Prince George and ordered staff at gunpoint to air the Leafs game instead of Vancouver versus California. He said that it was his son's NHL debut— Spencer was a local product, after all—and that he'd be interviewed between periods, something Brian had told him on the phone that afternoon. They complied, but as Roy Spencer left the building he was confronted by three RCMP officers. Spencer's dad was shot and killed during the standoff. Brian was given the news by Leafs GM Jim Gregory after the game.

After moving from the Leafs to the Islanders to the Penguins as a perennial favourite whose robust play and wild fighting style endeared him to hometown fans, Spencer struggled, as lots of players do, when he reached the other side of his life; there were a few assault charges after bar fights and a handful of DUIs. Eventually he settled in West Palm Beach near his hero, Dave Keon. But whereas the captain lived in a private enclave on the good side of the city, Spencer's home was a squalid trailer on the ragged edge of town in which he allegedly kept a baby grand piano whose width spanned the whole of the structure. According to journalist Tim Graham of the *Buffalo News,* "The site of the trailer was rural by Florida standards—it was only a small square of property—but it was very isolated and very sad-looking. It was exactly the kind of place that a drunk and a recluse would go to be alone."

If Graham's story on the late enforcer is any indication, Spencer had trouble holding down a job. He carried on an open relationship with a woman named Crystal (aka Diane Delena) from Fantasy Island Escorts. One evening Spencer stepped between her and a coke-addled client, Michael Dalfo. Whatever happened, Dalfo ended up dead and Spencer was charged with his murder. Delena corroborated the story after being given partial immunity, and for months Spencer sat in a jail cell staring at the death penalty. Three former players—the Sabres' Richard Martin, the Islanders' Gerry Hart, and Keon—were with him almost the entire way. Keon submitted his testimony near the later stages of the trial, which Spencer's team won due to a lack of evidence from the Crown.

Hart tried to reunite Spencer with his ex-wives (he had two; as well as five children from whom he was estranged), but he couldn't get the retired pugilist to commit to those parts of his life he'd left behind. Hart walked away, and with Martin still living up in Buffalo, Keon was left as the only close-range friend in Spencer's circle. While the two players occasionally saw each other, Spencer lived in his own orbit, and in the end West Palm Beach would prove no better a fit than anywhere else his life had brought him. Local detective George Mamak described Florida in the 1980s as "a killing zone," telling Graham, "Before crack [cocaine] it was all quiet by 2:00 a.m., but afterwards it was like *The Night of the Living Dead* till daybreak."

Eight months after his acquittal, Spencer was travelling at night with a friend down the notorious Avenue A in nearby Riviera Beach, looking for a coke buy. After securing the drugs, they'd parked the car up the road when another vehicle pulled up beside them. The driver held a gun out the window, demanding money. Spencer's friend, Greg Cook, gave the thieves three dollars, but the former player refused and was murdered in cold blood by construction worker Leon "Lump" Daniels, who claimed he was trying to get his money back after being ripped off during another coke deal that night. Some have speculated that the killing was retribution from Dalfo's family, but either way it was a sad and violent ending to an unhappy life. Despite the gulf that had widened between Spencer and Keon, the captain remained as loyal as he could be to his suffering friend. McKenny said that, when the body was brought to the morgue, they called Dave Keon to identify his murdered friend.

If Keon had been the last former teammate to see Spencer before his death, it wouldn't have been the first time. On the eve of Tim Horton's fatal crash, the Sabres defenceman sought out Keon after a game between the Leafs and Buffalo. He said goodbye to the captain on Church Street, visited the head office of his doughnut franchise, then died that night on the Queen Elizabeth highway.

There was also the item about how Keon had rushed to Bobby Baun's hotel room after the defenceman found himself in the middle of a violent nervous breakdown (he was eventually subdued by the captain and the veteran Horton), or the story, told by someone who made me promise not to name him, about how Keon had saved a teammate from financial disaster even though he was a spendthrift, as many players in those low-salaried days were. The late Pit (Hubert) Martin, who also came from Rouyn-Noranda, liked to tell a story about playing against his hero for the first time in the NHL, with Keon skating up to him and saying, "Just keep going, kid. You're gonna make it; I know you are." In Damien Cox and Gord Stellick's book about the last Leafs team to win the Cup, they wrote: "Bobby Haggert, the trainer on the '67 Leafs, recalled that when his wife died in 2001, he was surprised to pick up the phone and hear Keon's voice at the other end. 'I don't even know how he got my number,' said Haggert. 'I hadn't talked to him in twenty years. But it meant the world to me.'"

In the same *Weekend* column by Earl McRae that I'd found in the basement, the reporter wrote about his time working for the *Toronto Star* and reporting from the terminal ward of Sick Kids. McRae described a kid named Kenny who was "propped up on a bed when I met him, a stuffed tiger cradled in one arm, a photograph on the bedside table of his mom, dad, sister and himself. Kenny looked wonderful in the photo; a little, chubby guy with round cheeks ... and the sweetest smile. He was sitting on his daddy's knee.

"But the Kenny lying before me," wrote McCrae, "was a different child: pale and wasted, his hair all gone, his eyes flat and dull. It was shortly before Christmastime and Kenny's room was bright and festive with decorations. He didn't have his health, but he had his dream: he wanted to be a hockey player like his hero, Dave Keon. He wanted to grow up and play for the Leafs, to skate the way Keon skated, to win the Stanley Cup."

McRae continued the story: "I remember patting the boy on the head, telling him that it was a wonderful dream and how I was sure it would come true. Kenny smiled at the thought and I wished him well and said goodbye. At the next Leafs practice, I told Keon about the little boy who idolized him. Keon listened but said nothing.

"Kenny would have been twenty-two today, and, who knows, maybe thrilling us all in the uniform of the Maple Leafs. We'll never know. Shortly after New Year's, little Kenny died of leukemia. He was only seven years old. One of his last visitors was Dave Keon."

13

As November summoned early dark skies and the quick sting of winter, Roscoe continued to prey on the boy. When he wasn't sitting on him, forcing the boy to say "Leafs suck" over and over again, he was pulling the boy's toque off and holding his face to the ground so that he couldn't breathe. No one ever stopped to help. Once, a group of grade eights came over and asked if they could take a few shots. Roscoe told them to go fuck themselves.

Whenever the bully grew bored or tired, he mocked the boy for being a browner and a teacher's pet before calling him a loser and a knob and a spaz for liking the Leafs. The boy would become a man who would wonder whether it was this constant ridicule that steeled his devotion to his team, and whether, in the end, it was Roscoe's fault that his sporting fortunes were hitched to such a sad institution. Whatever the case, it made the boy want the Leafs to win more than ever, if only to smite the Roscoes of the world, putting in their place those who bullied others and who cheered for the Flyers and who had no moral compass in a world where good was supposed to beat evil.

After slagging the Leafs, Roscoe always made sure to talk about the Flyers and how great they were for winning the Stanley Cup. The boy lay there and took his medicine, saying nothing. Then, one afternoon, he opened his mouth. He had to. The bully was talking about the Flyers' winger, Reggie Leach.

The boy hated the Flyers as much as he hated anything, but one player he did not hate or could not hate was Reggie Leach. The boy thought that the player—people called him the "Riverton Rifle," because he came from Riverton, Manitoba—always seemed a little embarrassed whenever his team behaved horribly and terribly. While the rest of the Flyers yelled and shouted and facewashed and swarmed and brawled with their opponents, Leach was always found at the edge of the camera frame, floating backward toward centre ice. There was also something about his eyes—soft and curious, like a reluctant animal, thought the boy—that made the player seem vulnerable, although the boy would have called him "sad" or "unhappy," not knowing the other word. It was only later that the boy, after becoming a man, found out that Reggie had also been bullied at school, a little Native kid among Icelanders and Ukrainian kids who were bigger and more aggressive than he was. No wonder the Rifle couldn't stomach all the violence and fighting.

There was also something about the way Reggie Leach celebrated after scoring a goal that reminded the boy of Dave Keon. He didn't whoop or dance on his skates like Moose Dupont and he didn't drop to the ice acting like an amateur who'd never scored before. Instead, Reggie Leach in his post-goal moment looked as if he felt sorry for the goaltender, as if he wished there was another way to win without hurting the other team's feelings. The boy might have been reading too much into the player's behaviour, but he wasn't sure. He'd tried to squelch these feelings while watching the horrible terrible Flyers, but it was impossible. Sometimes the player looked lonely, and the boy wondered if he thought about what it might be like to play on another team that didn't do the things the horrible terrible Flyers did. One time during a brawl, the boy noticed the Rifle leaning over at the boards talking to the fans. Another time, the Flyers winger was standing at centre ice next to the Leafs captain. The two players were talking, and it was in that moment that the boy realized why he couldn't hate Reggie Leach the way he hated the other wretched Flyers: he was his team's Dave Keon. He played the game right no matter what was happening.

Because the Flyers had just beaten the pathetic Kansas City Scouts 10–0 at home, Roscoe had even more reason to crow about how good the Flyers were. To the boy, it was stupid—Kansas City were a rotten team—but at least it broke the monotony of their afternoon routine, and, besides, talking hockey was always good even under awful conditions. The boy had thought of doing this kind of thing before, imagining himself lost in a burned-out forest after a nuclear war trading Leafs stories with an old woodsman eating barbecued rat in a woodland clearing or explaining the game of hockey to green-skinned lizard-aliens who'd beamed him into their spaceship during one of those times he'd wandered out of his yard after being told not to. He also imagined being captured by bad men—terrorists, although not many people used that word back then—wearing dark hoods and robes who took the boy to a prison, where he gained his freedom after melting his captors' hearts by talking about the Leafs' stirring 1967 Cup victory over Montreal, and how Keon had been named the winner of the Conn Smythe Trophy. Roscoe was his captor, too, although whether the bully had a heart to melt, the boy wasn't sure.

As the schoolyard and the teachers' parking lot emptied, the thug announced, looking at no one but addressing the boy, who lay on his stomach, "Best faceoff man in the NHL? That's Bobby Clarke." Roscoe continued with his list:

"Best fighter: Dave 'The Hammer' Schultz.

"Best goalie: Bernie Parent.

"Best penalty killer: Bill Barber."

Then he said "Best defenceman: Moose Dupont" in a more boastful voice, mostly because he wasn't.

"And best scorer ..." He paused a moment for dramatic effect.

Failing to consider the result of his actions, the boy finished Roscoe's thought. He did this partly because he couldn't help himself and partly because he didn't want the thug saying someone stupid like Orest Kindrachuk or Tom Bladon or Ross Lonsberry or Terry Crisp.

The boy told him: "Reggie Leach."

For a moment, nothing happened. The boy lay there and waited. He thought he could feel Roscoe's weight ease off him just a little, a slight shift in movement, legs sliding back a few inches, haunches lifted.

"And best scorer ..." the thug repeated.

The boy said nothing.

"And best scorer ..." he said, a little louder.

The boy answered him: "The Rifle."

"Looks like you're finally seeing things my way."

"I like the Rifle," said the boy.

"He's better than that faggot Lafleur and better than that dago Esposito and better than that gaylord Bobby Orr."

"You can't fake talent like that," said the boy, repeating something he'd heard Bob Goldham say about Börje Salming.

"You saying he's faking?" said Roscoe.

"No, I meant the opposite. I said you can't fake it. That move he made around Larry Robinson two weeks ago on *Hockey Night in Canada*? It was like a barracuda going through the arms of a giant squid," he said, surprising himself with the image.

"A barracuda? I like that. You're not so useless after all," he told the boy.

"Thanks."

"Though you're still pretty fucking useless," he said, swatting the back of his head.

"Okay," said the boy.

"What else do you like about the Rifle?" asked the bully.

"His shot, especially."

"What else?"

"He's a quick skater, and strong, too."

"What else?" asked Roscoe.

"He's pretty dominant on the power play. Scored twelve goals last year."

"You know that?"

"Yeah," said the boy, not knowing how anyone who was a fan of Reggie Leach would not.

"Okay, what else?"

"Well," said the boy.

"Well, what?"

"Well."

"WELL WHAT?" he said, punching the boy in the back.

"Well. He seems kind of sad."

The boy waited to be punched again. Maybe karate-chopped in the neck. Maybe spat on. Maybe kneed in the balls. Instead, the bully came off his prey. He stood above him.

"What do you mean?"

"I dunno," said the boy. "Sometimes after he scores, he looks sad. For himself and for the goalie."

"That's stupid."

"Also, sometimes he looks as if maybe he's too sad or something to even celebrate scoring," the boy continued. "You saw him after that goal against the Habs?"

"I saw it."

"Well, he didn't even celebrate. Not at all. Besides, Clarke is always chirping. Barber's always diving everywhere. Schultz and Saleski are always fighting. But Leach doesn't do any of that. He just plays."

"You make him sound like he's a wimp or something," said Roscoe, putting his foot on the boy's back.

"I don't mean to," said the boy. "Besides, he's not a wimp. He's tough, obviously. I mean, he's playing in the NHL. All I'm saying is that sometimes not even the best things in the world can be enough if you're sad. Maybe that's why he is how he is. I don't know."

The boy lay there a moment. Roscoe turned and walked away. His head was down and his steps seemed heavy.

14

Day after day, I thought about trying to find my hero. Having avoided formal training in journalism and not blessed with the ability to ambush a stranger as a way to a story, I'd always just written, and while this afforded me a certain rogue freedom, it also made me uncertain about how to move down the road I was now required to travel. I decided that booking a plane ticket south was still a reach, and besides, I couldn't tell whether McKenny had said what he'd said—"Keon'll do it. I mean, he has to"—because he was a good guy, or whether talking to the captain would be as difficult as it had been for other journalists wanting to tell the player's story.

But then an avenue opened up. Through *Hockey Night in Canada*'s Joel Darling, I placed a call to Dave's son—Dave Keon Jr.—the near spitting image of his father who'd been a Gardens' goal judge for years and had recently assumed the mantle of public relations director for the National Hockey League. Dave Jr. had seen Joel at an NHL function, and he'd asked him, "So what's up with this book about my dad that this guy is writing?" Joel said, "I don't know; why don't you ask him yourself?" before facilitating an exchange of numbers. If anyone could grasp my estrangement from my hero, I thought Dave Jr. could, having fallen out with his father through the early 1990s before reconciling and growing closer.

As gently as he could, Dave Jr. told me that getting his father to talk would be a futile effort, and that even if I did manage to get an interview, there was no guarantee he'd produce any insight. He said that a writer had recently been dispatched to his father by a local sports publication. Keon Sr. told his son that it was "the same old shit, more or less." I told myself that it would be different with me, but, then again, I didn't know. Maybe the other writer had told him what I'd tell him—that I was his biggest fan and greatest admirer—but in the end it didn't matter. I'd have to say something he hadn't heard before, something real and true and moving. I remembered Howie's words: "The whole focus is on something you did or didn't do fifty years ago." For Keon, it must have seemed like another lifetime. But for me it seemed like yesterday.

Through Dave Jr. and Dave's cousin, Jody, who, it turned out, was a fan of my music by way of a close friend, writer Angie Abdou, I was connected to Jim Keon, the captain's younger brother by six years. If the senior Keon had a reputation for being guarded or ill-humoured or

bitter—all of these words had been used to describe him—
Jim was an effortless storyteller, and open to any nature of
discussion about his family, his brother, and life in Rouyn-
Noranda. "The family is a hundred percent behind what
you're doing," he told me. "It's an important story that
deserves to be told." He also said, "Sometimes my brother
comes across as a little guarded because he feels like, at
times, he's been burned in the past," but then suggested
that I keep trying. "Once you get to know him, David is
great company," he told me. Still, how I was supposed to
establish this closeness or confidence was beyond me.

I moved on with a certain weary duty, trying to collect
stories and information about Dave Keon with the single-
mindedness of a bedder stuffing a duvet. On the morning
of the city's gorgeous first snowfall, I shuffled through a
set of papers, finding a list of numbers scribbled in dark
ink. Laying the list in my lap, I picked up the phone. I
called Harry Neale.

Neale had been a Maple Leafs broadcaster and
longtime NHL and WHA coach, but he'd also been
a partner in the Keon-Harris Hockey School, which
the captain had run with Billy Harris, his teammate
throughout the 1960s. I'd met Harris a few times. Once,
during a live interview on CBC's *Benmergui Live,* the former
Leaf and 1974 Team Canada WHA coach elbowed me
and gestured to a screen with the name of the show
written on it. He pointed to the word "Live" and said, "I
know what that means. But what does that mean?" while
pointing at the host's name.

I grew up in Etobicoke with Harris's son—a slight, wispy-haired kid named Billy Junior—where we spent grades six, seven, and eight at Dixon Grove Middle School. Despite being the world's biggest Leafs fan, I hardly ever talked with Billy about his dad, or his dad's friendship with Keon. Instead we worked on science projects together, wrote skits, and played baseball. Dialing Neale's number in upstate New York, I thought of the school's vast running track landscaped with a huge swatch of grass and baseball diamonds at one end. At my own kids' school a field had been bulldozed to make room for another building that would generate income and raise property value. It was no wonder McKenny had said what he'd said about kids not caring anymore. Without great parcels of land on which to run and throw and skate, it was impossible to know sports at an eyeline to the ground. It was from this perspective that I first experienced games—skidding chin to the earth trying to catch this or stop that or make a game-saving sprawl that left a green stripe along the middle of my shirt. The taste of schoolyard grass was still fresh in the cavern of my senses, and for a moment it returned with the memory of Billy Junior and the joy of our shared youth. Then, suddenly and strangely, the sweetness of this memory turned sour—but before I knew why a spry voice picked up on the other end of the line. I said hello to Harry Neale.

I told the coach that I was writing about Keon, who'd played for Neale during his first year with the WHA's Minnesota Fighting Saints (he'd also owned a Parry Sound fishing camp with him in the off-season).

Then Harry—repeating something I was sure I'd heard on Leafs broadcasts whenever the subject of the captain was raised—said, "What Davey Keon did as a hockey player was remarkable. These days you have defensive and offensive specialists, but Keon was both and all of these things. He played the whole game against the team's best line, he played when they were ahead by a goal, and he played when they needed to score. He played on the power play and the penalty kill. He played the first minute and the last minute. He was great in freewheeling games and he was great when the games were tough. There are few forwards—if any—who are as good playing offence as they are at defending." Harry's words reminded me of something I'd read in Stephen Cole's great book, *The Last Hurrah,* about the 1967 season. He quoted Allan Stanley, who used to organize defenceman-only gatherings outside the rink, and who said, "Davey was always thinking defence. Leafs defencemen used to go out together after practice; no forwards. But sometimes we'd invite Davey. Horton would say, 'Ah, he's almost a defenceman anyway.'"

Neale acquired Keon for his WHA team after the 1974/75 season, but it wasn't the first time the new league had presented Keon with an opportunity. In 1972 he was selected in the WHA draft by a prospective Ontario club that ended up becoming the Ottawa Nationals. The team's owner, Doug Michel, had hoped to sign Keon as a way of seeking revenge on Harold Ballard, who'd mocked Michel's attempt to secure the rights to use Maple Leaf Gardens as the Nationals' home rink. Stories suggest that there was some traction during discussions with Keon's agent, Mike Elik. A clandestine meeting was held at Pearson airport to discuss terms, and, according to the book *Left Wing and a Prayer,* Keon was open to the idea, even hinting that a few other Leafs might jump leagues as well. Keon wanted a five-year deal at $150,000 plus twenty-five percent of the Nationals. While Elik convinced a bank to guarantee the yearly dollars, Michel committed only a small personal amount, which became a red flag for Keon's lawyer, Jim Stevens. Still, club stock options, home seats for games, and a company car were included in the deal, and after Keon's people asked for and received a $200,000 guarantee from Elik, everything seemed in place to make Keon the centrepiece of the new team. Keon had asked for a $50,000 advance, and a bank cheque was immediately produced. Elik travelled to Toronto in a rented Cadillac, where Keon, without the presence of his agent or lawyer, signed a letter of intent. Outraged that this meeting had gone down, Stevens accused Elik of seducing his client and wanted the agreement torn up. Both sides continued the back-and-forth, with Stevens requesting that Keon be paid a million dollars if the team wasn't operating by December 13, 1972. The deal collapsed. Elik ended up being out $50,000 and Keon re-signed with the Leafs.

After the mess in Ottawa, Minnesota was a natural destination for the captain, given his relationship with Harry. When I asked Neale about Keon's attitude to the new, less established league, the former coach had this to say: "Almost immediately he embraced our team, his new team. From the first practice, he put pressure on teammates to perform, and when he spoke, everyone listened. He was probably the most cerebral player I ever coached. Ask any defenceman and they'll tell you that he kept an inventory in his head of what he'd done against them, how he'd beaten—or not beaten—them. He was brilliant at pulling the puck in on the defenceman, but he could also outrace you. Not only that, but he had his angles down perfectly and you could never fool him. He was always thinking, always. His eyes started whirling and you could see it right there between the lines."

Then I asked Neale about the captain's post-retirement absence from the Leafs. "It was clear that Keon had great pride in his Leafs career," he said. "Nobody was as proud, I don't think. But he's still bitter about how it ended. When they have reunions organized by Leafs alumni, he's more likely to show up than if they're organized by the team. He doesn't talk about his career because it still hurts him that they did what they did. It runs very deep in him. Is that healthy or good? I don't know. He's down there in Florida and I'm overdue to go see him. I don't know how many visitors he has. He likes the company, and we have a good time together. But we never—repeat, never—talk about the Leafs." Finally, I asked the former coach if he could describe Keon's attitude toward his playing career in one word. There was a long pause before Harry spoke.

"Heartbroken," he said.

After ending the call with Neale I started another, phoning Dale Tallon, who'd grown up with the Keons in northern Quebec. Both players had been born in the jagged rockscape of Rouyn-Noranda, twin mining cities gouged out of the mineral-rich terrestrial fold between the northeast border of Ontario and Quebec, fifty kilometres from Kirkland Lake, its hockey-mad provincial opposite. Keon was the first NHLer from the area—thirty-seven players would follow, including Tallon—and both families lived on Murdoch Street—named after James Murdoch, the founder of Noranda Mines—a cul-de-sac that ended at the gates through which the miners marched every morning before descending into the earth. The Keons and the Tallons were black Irish who'd grown up in the heart of French Canada, Anglo kids who spoke French in a café au lait culture that mixed Gallic and Anglo influences. "In the beginning the English players had all the brawn while the French had the skill," said Tallon, "but after a while one rubbed off on the other until we were producing tough skaters who could score: players like Keon, Kent Douglas, Réjean Houle, and the Connolly brothers. Even as Anglos, we loved going to French parties; they were always the most fun and no one minded. We'd play in Kirkland Lake against guys like Tommy Webster, Mickey Redmond, and Bob Murdoch, and the crowd would stand up and sing 'O Canada' at the top of their lungs like it was some kind of political gesture, but half of us were Anglo and half of us were French. In that sense, we were more Canadian than any team. We were two sets of people getting along. You couldn't see the dividing line no matter how hard you looked."

Another characteristic shared by the two men was the fact that, while most local players—like Houle, Jacques Lapierrière, and Serge Savard, who used to watch Tim Horton and Moose Vasko play road hockey outside his bedroom window in nearby Duparquet—were streamed into the Habs, the city's de facto parent team, both Keon and Tallon ended up playing in English Canada. Keon became more iconic because he captained the Maple Leafs and won four Stanley Cups, but Tallon will be remembered— fondly by some, less so by others—as the first-ever draft pick in the Vancouver Canucks' franchise history. He was chosen second overall, a draft slot determined by a large novelty gaming wheel spun in the Parenteau Room of Montreal's Queen Elizabeth Hotel on June 11, 1970. The Canucks missed out on selecting the Sabres' star forward Gilbert Perreault, a twist of fortune that slowed the team's emergence, even though Tallon would become a two-time all star and an occasionally prolific scorer. Still, he was chosen ahead of Philadelphia's Reggie Leach and Toronto's Darryl Sittler, both of whom became their team's respective franchise players. In the end, the Canucks dealt the tall, dark-haired defenceman to Chicago for Suitcase Smith and King Kong Korab, suggesting that, had he acquired a colourful nickname during his stay, Dale Tallon might have remained a Canuck a little while longer.

Tallon's father, Stan, was an important figure in the development of northern hockey, which produced a

stream of players who helped mature the NHL from a
city league played by few into an organization built on
a wave of immigrant kids who came from small places,
select varsity boys giving way to players with twisted-
vowel last names who skated with relentless fervour. As
Jim Keon put it, "Rouyn-Noranda was a melting pot, but
it also wasn't classist, despite the presence of the mine.
The children of miners went to school with the mine
manager's daughter and the doctor's son, and back then,
if you put on airs or were a fraud, people saw through it
quickly. This was especially true in hockey, where there
was zero class system. Everyone was on equal footing, no
matter how you grew up."

The north produced nearly one-third of the entire
skating corps of the 1940s and 50s, the area's prosperity
having drawn countless new families from every tough
pocket of the world to hardscrabble towns dug out of the
Canadian wilderness. If rugged Midwest ball diamonds in
new American territories gave baseball a birthing ground
out of the Great Depression, it was the frozen church
courtyards and edge-of-the-lake rinks of Temiskaming
and points east that produced an entire generation of
players. And none was as productive as Rouyn-Noranda.

Dale Tallon remembered his dad as "a man's man, a
great athlete who gave everything he had and whose only
fault was that he maybe didn't leave enough left over for
himself." Part of his organizing genius lay in gathering
whoever was willing to play and giving them a chance,
especially troubled and nearly poor kids, at a time when

the disenfranchised were often victimized. "Dad liked troubled kids," said Tallon, "and sometimes he'd anoint them as stick boys as a way of getting them onto the team or at least feeling like part of the team. They could earn a little money, feel a little measure of self-worth. I think he saw R-N as a sort of oasis, a place where everybody would be viewed equally, and out of that came this incredible force of players. In great hockey towns, it's never just a select few that give a place a reputation. It's the overall community: the Kiwanis clubs, the volunteers, the drivers, the teachers. In our case, it was people like Jacques Lapierrière's older brother, Gilles, and my dad who kept it all together. There were lots of players whose families didn't have a lot and who didn't show promise at first—players like the Bordeleau brothers [Jean-Pierre, Paulin, and Christian, all big leaguers]—but because the spirit around the community was so positive, they were given a chance. Someone like Fern Tessier, for instance, was always in trouble, but my dad got him a job working on a brick pile. After that, things took care of themselves. Fern credits my dad for getting him straight. There were lots like him. Lots."

Tallon's dad worked for the Montreal Canadiens, and every year he'd take a few busloads of kids down to Montreal's Junior Canadiens' camp to get them skates and sticks and show them the big city, an often out-of-reach place for northerners of limited means. Because R-N produced so many players, NHLers were around all the time, more so when you considered that half of them had summer jobs in the mines or were doing other things around the region. "Pit Martin used to take care of me as a kid," said Dale, "and when I was nine years old, Scotty Bowman wrote me a letter at my dad's behest encouraging me to keep playing. Kids are sometimes forced into hockey in maybe not the greatest environment, but if I could sum up my experience in one word, it would be 'joy.' The climate of hockey in that city made me the person I am today.

"One of my favourite memories," Tallon continued, "came when I was thirteen years old. My dad said, 'C'mon, our team is going to play the Kirkland Lake Lions tonight and you should come along.' I thought I was going to be the stick boy, but when we got to the rink my dad turned to me and said, 'We're short-handed, I think we're going to need you to skate for us,' even though everyone was about two or three years older than me. Before I got dressed, he told me that, whatever happened, I was absolutely not to tell my mother, because she wouldn't have liked me playing against bigger kids in another city.

"Turned out I had a good game—I got a goal and an assist—but on the last play of the game I was suckered by a big kid coming across the ice who forearmed me and broke my nose. It was forty-five miles home, and I held a bag of snow on my face the whole time. My dad said, 'I'll get you out of the house early tomorrow and send you to old Doc Turner. He'll fix you up, and when you come home from school, tell your mom you got into a fight in the schoolyard.' It seemed like a pretty good plan, and that's how it all ended up playing out.

"But unbeknownst to me or my dad, Mom had gone out that day and bought a transistor radio. We'd just started getting CJKL on the radio, and after turning it on, what she heard was 'Thirteen-year-old Dale Tallon got a goal and an assist last night against the Kirkland Lake Lions.' When I came home that day with two black eyes and told her about the fight I hadn't been in, she looked and me and said, 'You little lying bastard.' It was bad, but for the old man it was twice as worse."

After listening to these stories—I could have stayed on the line all day, and Tallon, it seemed, could have happily indulged me—I asked the GM about his awareness of Keon while growing up. He told me that by the time he started to play, Keon was already a heroic figure. "It was his skating—such quickness, and what people today would have called 'core strength,' but which didn't really exist back then." In Tallon's eyes, his reputation hadn't dimmed in the slightest, particularly since Keon came home a few times a year to tend to his parents' grave. "They've got an arena named after Dave in Rouyn and a big poster of him there. He goes back more than he does to Toronto, and everyone treats him normally. I don't think there's the baggage up there that maybe there is in the big city. He's an important part of the history of the place, and you know the French: they're good at celebrating all that, at recognizing the contributions of those who came before."

When I asked the old Canuck to describe the arena, he seemed surprised.

"You want me to describe it?"

"Yes, if you don't mind."

"Well, I could, sure," he said. "But you know, wouldn't it better if you saw it yourself?"

"Yes, I guess it would."

"Well, why don't you?" said Dale Tallon.

"Why don't I what?"

"Why don't you go up there?"

It was a question for which I had no reasonable answer.

PART TWO

I'm coming back to look for you.
—Rush, "Finding My Way"

15

On a bright fall morning I awoke early, shouted to my kids that I was leaving for Quebec, kissed my wife, then rode in a taxi to Toronto's island airport, where I boarded a Porter flight to Timmins. Upon landing, I rented a car from one of the handful of desks in the tiny airport. "Going to Ruin, are ya?" the attendant asked. "Yeah," I said, "in more ways than one."

I drove east, the great October sunshine bathing the Precambrian Shield in the fullness of light. Signs appeared for places like Matheson, Ramore, South Porcupine, Matachewan, Swastika, Nighthawk Lake, Iroquis Falls, Matagami, and Moonbeam, and for the first forty minutes I followed a pickup truck whose licence plate read BIGSTEVE. The land was mostly flat and coated with coniferous trees, and every now and then a small car with the words HEAVY LOAD brassiered across its fender approached from the other lane, followed by an enormous tractor-trailer carrying a huge round disc like the bottom half of a space capsule—the kind of thing that, should it become loosed from the truck, would thud violently before spinning across the surrounding acreage, wrecking anything in its path, were there anything to wreck. Passing a rest stop, I saw a group of large, moustached men in coveralls smoking and talking—miners on break or furlough, I figured—and later on I'd occasionally see more large men at construction sites and even more standing beside their trucks at the roadside. I'd been astonished before by the sheer scale of the country, but it had been a while. Here I was once again reminded of the extravagant mass of the land, as well as the size of tools and the build of the people required to live in it.

Closer to Kirkland Lake the country began to roll a little, and soon the trees lost their fur, giving way to stands of leafless Jack pines, balsams, and white birches whose pale bark glowed under the midday sun. I passed a sign with silhouettes of a black bear and a moose, marking the point at land's height where all rivers and streams began to flow north to the Arctic Ocean. The highway swooped then fell—then swooped and fell some more— revealing vistas of lighted wood, and when it wasn't doing that it was revealing blue-black autumnal lakes, one after another, with names like Bear or Elk or Mud or Trout or Wood or Deer, and occasionally a solitary loon floating two-toned in the unrippled peace of the waters. Feeling foolish for having driven past most of this, I pulled the car down a gravel road to the foot of a lake, where I stood with my hands in my coat pockets absorbing the beauty of the scene—a dark forest with the rumour of wolf and lynx peering out at me on slumped bellies; pure, cold lake water reaching a pebbled beach still wet with an overnight kiss of snow; a crooked stand of jagged treetops waving in time to its own low rhythm—all of which made me feel almost embarrassingly Canadian, which made me feel more Canadian still.

Climbing back into the car, my mind drifted into the warmth of fantasy. I returned to the conversation I'd imagined taking place with the captain in Florida at his favourite Chili's or Applebee's or Denny's, or maybe an Olive Garden patio looking out at the sea. I thought I might win some credibility by telling Dave Keon about my trip to play hockey in Mongolia, which I'd done in 2002. I would tell him a funny story about how I'd found mention of the Leafs in a local newspaper, whose offices I'd visited with my friend Pujee. I imagined Keon looking at me with suspicion. "They play hockey in Mongolia?" he'd say.

"Yes, they do," I'd reply. "I've seen it for myself."

Keon would shake his head and raise a finger, at which point the server would deliver a basket of chicken poppers—I'm not sure what chicken poppers are, but it seemed like the kind of thing we'd be eating—and two green-bottled Rolling Rocks, chips of ice melting down their necks. The day was hot and the beers were cold. I would start telling the story. At least that's how I imagined it going.

I would tell Keon that I'd gone to Mongolia to make a film, *The Hockey Nomad,* about hockey around the world. Maybe he'd heard of it, maybe not. In Ulan Bator I'd met Pujee, whose real name was Choijiljav Purevdavaa (Keon would laugh at the name; at least I hoped he would), through a fellow named Herb Shoveller (maybe the captain would laugh at Herb's name, too) who came from London, Ontario, and whose team had travelled to UB from Hong Kong for an all-Asian rec friendly. I would tell Keon how "Pujee drove a nearly destroyed Jeep whose side and rear-view mirrors were long ago pillaged and sold for scraps." The scraps, I'd tell him, "had been left to waste in one of the myriad rubble-filled craters and dead-brick mountains that give UB the look of a city stressed by industrial holocaust. Still, this torn grey canvas was Pujee's home, and as we drove through the city's tilted streets and dirt hills"—at this point I thought I might have sounded like I was quoting my own writing, but I continued—"Pujee pointed through the windshield to the deep bright snow ringing the edge of the city, the Skylab and Let It Be discotheques (two dance halls built after Mongolia's liberation from its Soviet masters), and the two outdoor hockey rinks that glazed the city. It was these rinks, along with the Buddhist monasteries and snorting horses patrolling the streets," I would say, "that made UB feel barely breathing, but breathing all the same." For sure I sounded like I was quoting my own writing. But I didn't think the captain would mind. I continued telling the story in the quiet of the moving car.

I would explain to him how Pujee had fallen in love with the game after watching young Russian workers play on natural ice from the balcony of his family's apartment. I would say: "One afternoon I went with him to the train station, where he passed a fistful of American dollars to a stick-buying friend bound for the region's nearest sporting goods store in Irkutsk, Siberia, ten hours away. Two weeks later he returned with a bouquet of thirty new Sherwoods, the tools with which the Mongolian National Hockey League would start their eighth season.

"A few evenings later," I would continue, "Pujee and I were wandering through a half-built apartment block when we came upon a small lineup of people waiting for an appearance by the Dalai Lama, who, like me, was bunking in one of UB's small, newish, Western-style hotels." I imagined Keon's eyes lighting up a little as he pulled on the neck of his beer. "After discovering that the Holy Man was about to make an appearance, Mike Downie—my friend and the film's director—did what any savvy director of any hockumentary would have done: he pushed me into the lineup, muttering something about 'Buddhism! Number One!' and 'Star quality' and 'Taking shots on the Dalai Lama!'" At this point I imagined Keon pushing a short laugh out of his nose, then drawing the sleeve of his shirt across his face.

"I asked Mike if I should hold my stick while waiting in the lineup," I'd tell Keon, "and he said, 'Brilliant idea!,' imagining, no doubt, that the Lama would stop in his tracks, fit my gleaming Easton between his hands, and impulsively work a cracked-brick puck through the city streets. Mike disappeared for a moment, then returned with my excalibur, proving that while getting to travel the world playing hockey was pretty special, having one's own equipment valet was kind of exceptional, too."

I would keep talking. "The Lama finally strode out of the hotel, shining his brilliant smile before being whisked off to a waiting town car. As the driver inched down the driveway and cruised to where the lineup started, a pulse of joy carried through the crowd. The car moved slowly so that everyone could take in the great man, who sat in the passenger side, tipping his head, waving and smiling. It was really quite a scene—one set of dancing eyes playing upon another—and as the sky darkened into a dark blue brightened only by the thick falling snow, it actually felt like a decent time to cross paths with a living deity, despite the camera's chassis whirring in my ear," I'd say. "Then as the Lama passed me," I would continue, checking to make sure the captain was still engaged in the story (he was), "I did what any red-blooded Canadian would have done: I thrust my stick at him, or rather, his car. I was hoping that the Holy One might bless my graphite one-piece, and as the blade curved across his sightline, I saw him lower his head and, I sensed, incant a small prayer, perhaps an ode to an Easton. For the next few months after returning home, I carried my stick with a blessed-by-God permanence, pretty much shooting at the net every chance I got. And then, one day, the stick exploded at the heel. I realized that maybe it wasn't a prayer that the Lama had incanted after all."

I imagined the captain laughing some more, before saying, "Well, you certainly have some wild stories. The kind I've never heard before." Possibly exceeding my bounds, but going ahead all the same, I imagined telling him, "But that's not what I wanted to say." The captain would fold his hands on the table. "All right. What is it you wanted to tell me exactly?"

I knew that, should this moment come to pass, I'd want to tell him more than just an amusing anecdote about my time spent in northeastern Asia. But I'd hold steady for the moment. I imagined saying to the captain, "I wanted to tell you about the Leafs, how I found them in Mongolia." I envisioned landing heavily on that last word. Keon would turn over his hand. He would tell me to proceed.

"On our second or third day there," I'd say, "we visited the local newspaper, which boasted the city's largest and most comprehensive sports sections. The first thing one of the young Mongolian sportswriters did upon meeting me was produce a copy of their September issue, which had prognostications on the upcoming (2005) NHL season. He found the page that pegged the order of finish for all the teams, giggling to himself while dragging his finger to the Maple Leafs." At this point I imagined looking out over the road to the beach and then to the ocean, thrilled that I was where I was and with whom. I finished the story.

"They'd predicted the Leafs would finish in last place. The journalist looked at me to see if he'd gotten a rise. I shook my head and told Pujee to tell him, 'It doesn't bode well when guys twenty thousand miles away are picking your home team to finish last.'" Keon would laugh at the story and I would laugh along with him. Then: more beers. Lots more, I told myself. In a perfect world, I'd wander home drunk and amazed that our meeting had gone as well as it had. That's how it would go down.

16

After an inconsistent start to the year, the 74/75 Leafs suddenly fell into the doldrums, stumbling through a four-game losing run, beginning with a lead-footed 5–2 loss to Vancouver. In the boy's mind, this loss was less acceptable than most, because to him the Canucks were little more than a strange new team from elsewhere. It was hard enough getting his head around the fact that a big city existed so far away in the same country where he lived, let alone a hockey team that came from there. The Canucks also had lots of players whose names were hard to pronounce: Orland Kurtenbach, Jocelyn Guevremont, Chris Oddleifson (whose jaw, said the *Toronto Star,* had been broken five times), Ron Sedlbauer, Larry Goodenough, Dennis Ververgaert, and Sheldon Kannegiesser, whose name vexed even himself, becoming "Sheldon Kane" for the purposes of selling houses in California during his retirement. Because of the time difference, the Canucks were hardly ever on *Hockey Night in Canada,* making them a mere rumour of a team. Later on, when the 80s version of the club took to wearing bizarre yellow and black V-neck sweaters, it seemed to the boy as if they were simply playing to their alien nature.

In the 1980s the Leafs traded with Vancouver for the first time, dealing Tiger Williams and Jerry Butler to the Canucks for Rick Vaive and Bill Derlago. The new Leafs were never able to lead them out of the wilderness, while Tiger ended up being a force that carried Vancouver to their first Cup appearance in 1982; it was an expansion team that achieved what the post-expansion Leafs never could. Still, if the Rick Vaive acquisition hadn't translated into a Leafs post-season slot, he was nonetheless a larger-than-life—and also just plain large—figure in Toronto sports. His slapshot had an impossibly broad windup—soccer analysts might have called it "audacious" or "cynical"—that seemed to be as much about breaking the glass as beating the goalie. As a result, the PEI winger is primarily known for doing what no other Leafs player had done before: score fifty goals, albeit in the points-happy era of the 1980s.

The boy would become a man whose favourite Rick Vaive story would be told to him by Curtis Joseph, then a young goalie with the St. Louis Blues. Growing up a Leafs fan, Joseph was thrilled to face Vaive in his first pro game at Maple Leaf Gardens, during which the square-headed winger came roaring over the blue line with the puck.

After winding up—his stick nearly scraping the mouldy struts of the rink's ancient ceiling—Vaive fired with such velocity that Cujo was unable to trace the puck's flight path. "I heard it hit me," said the goalie, "but the force was so great that I ended up being knocked over on my back in the crease." Vaive's momentum had carried him all the way to the goal, and after the whistle blew he was lying on top of Joseph in the net. "I could see his face through the mask," said Cujo, "a face I'd seen on television all those years. He looked at me and said, 'Nice save, kid.' That's when I realized I was playing in the NHL."

The '82 Canucks maintained their oddly-named-players tradition, filling out a roster that included the densely eyebrowed Garth Butcher, and, for comic effect, Jiri Bubla. There was also Andy Schliebener, which sounded like what happened when you crossed a Kannegiesser with a Sedlbauer, as well as Moe Lemay, a name more likely to be found on a casino lounge napkin. Perhaps Vancouver's most talented, and credible, player was the fleet young Italo-Canadian forward Tony Tanti, whose pro career had begun as inauspiciously as any player's in history. Once Tanti signed his bonus with the Canucks, he bought a sports car. After driving it off the lot he picked up his girlfriend and headed out to dinner. When he pulled up in front of the restaurant an attendant came over and asked if he wanted the car parked, so the rookie tossed him the keys. After dinner, he asked the maître d' to summon the valet, and was greeted with a curious look. It turned out the restaurant had no valet service. The car was never found, and Tanti played nearly a quarter season before making back the money.

The Leafs' defeat at the hands of the Canucks was followed by an 8–5 loss to Pittsburgh and a 6–0 defeat to the New York Islanders, who, it turned out, weren't even from New York, but a place called Long Island. The run continued with a loss to the horrible terrible Flyers, 6–3, before the Leafs finally beat the pathetic Washington Capitals, who'd joined the league at the same time Kansas City did. Even though the game ended 7–1, it was hardly an indicator that things were getting better, considering that the Caps would win only eight games that year, in the process setting a futility mark for lowest-winning percentage ever: .131.

The thing that bugged the boy most about the Leafs' losing skein had more to do with what was happening off the ice than on it, although, sure, what was happening on it wasn't good, either. After the Leafs won only five games through October and November, Harold Ballard—a fat, grouchy man with angry glasses and skin like greying lettuce—began saying terrible things about the team, singling out Dave Keon for being more terrible than the rest. On the morning of November 20, the boy sat at the breakfast nook eating Cap'n Crunch and reading the paper. The story in the *Globe* started: "The president of the Toronto Maple Leafs says his players should be ashamed to walk the streets and face the citizens of Toronto, so disgusting is their play." Ballard called the Leafs a "stinking exhibition" and singled out Keon's Swedish winger, Inge

Hammarström, of whom the owner said, "You could send him in a corner with six eggs in his pocket and he wouldn't break any of them." If that wasn't bad enough, he said the Leafs were out of shape and "too fat," which, to the boy, was a little like Jabba the Hutt telling Mark Spitz he might consider doing the odd pushup.

In the *Star*'s sports section, Ballard also questioned Keon's leadership, saying, "I don't think Keon is the fiery leader we need." This made the boy stiffen with anger, but it got worse. "We could use a whipman, a Bobby Clarke type," groused the tyrant, "someone who could fire the team up by word as by deed. There's nobody here in this organization to provide spirit and leadership except King Clancy. The veterans should be raising hell with the kids and getting them going."

The boy thought that criticizing the team was one thing—Ballard did it all the time on television, waving his arms around, his jowls shaking and his lip curled in disgust—but comparing Keon with Clarke was dirty business, considering that the Flyers were the Leafs' sworn enemies and league nemesis, setting the team penalty record that year, a record they already owned. Not only that, but in the 6–3 loss to Philadelphia, Clarke had proved to be dirtier than anyone on the team, spearing Leafs defenceman Rod Seiling in the face. In classic chickenshit Philly style—the boy, of course, wouldn't have used the word "chickenshit," knowing that swearing was wrong—winger Bill Barber jumped in after Clarke's spear, punching Seiling as the defenceman threw his hands to his face, wondering whether he'd been blinded. Even worse, a few days later Clarke called Seiling and said he was sorry, which the boy thought he must have done while sniggering behind his hand in an apartment filled with other Flyers—Dupont, Bridgman, Saleski, Schultz—all of them drinking and smoking as their captain covered the receiver to stifle the sound of their cruel laughter. If the Leafs modelled their style after Keon's hard work, savvy, and honest hustle, the Flyers were the Flyers because of Bobby Clarke, at whose feet monsters gathered. A few years earlier the Flyers captain had been chosen over Keon to represent Canada in the 1972 Summit Series, even though the captain had had a better year. And now Harold Ballard was praising him, saying he was better than Keon, and that a world ruled by Roscoes was okay.

Ballard's comments sickened the boy. The only saving grace was knowing that Keon would steel himself from being affected. He played the game the way he played it, and no lardhead with ears like hideous mushrooms and a drooping-testicles chin was going to make him change. The boy's notion was confirmed in the following game against Pittsburgh, whose name—the Penguins—the boy had always thought was funny. Even sillier was the Penguins' crest, which showed a laughing bird wearing a toque tipped back on its head and a scarf tailfinning behind him. The boy wondered what Penguins players like Steve Durbano—a player as horrible terrible as anyone on the Flyers—or Dennis Owchar—who looked like a criminal on drugs with uncombed hair and cracked teeth—must have thought while bayonetting their stick at another player, all the while knowing they had a gaylord-looking ice bird on their crest. It couldn't have been good. Then again, maybe that's how come the Penguins had so many fighters. Maybe they were just mad at their sweaters.

Like the Sabres, the Penguins had some lame players, with names like Bob Stumpf and Nelson Debenedet and Ron Schock, but they also had Pierre Larouche and Syl Apps, who was related to the former Leafs captain of the same name. Still, they all could have been called Apps and not stopped Keon, who, from the first batting of the puck, skated as if carving his full name plus middle initial in the rink, his rushes fevered and determined in an attempt to prove his owner wrong. In the game's opening moments he powered his way through the Pens' defence before being dragged by two Penguins to the ice. Bruce Hood's arm shot in the air and pointed to centre ice, signalling a penalty shot. The Gardens crowd—many of whom had watched Keon mature from a boy into a man, blossoming from a checking centre into a league-scoring star—sat there as still as an animal suddenly noticed by a larger animal, worried that any movement might disrupt the forces that had quietly gathered over the moment. Ballard and his sidekick, a man named King Clancy, whom the boy liked a lot even though he was Ballard's friend, watched from an opening that had been dug out of a wall in the end golds in a room that people called "the bunker." Before taking the penalty shot the captain leaned on his stick at centre ice, his back to the Leafs owner. The boy thought that maybe he was sticking out his bum a little bit more than usual. But maybe not. The boy couldn't be sure.

He was almost certain that Dave Keon was going to use his backhand, which he executed like no other player before him. Years later, the boy would marvel at what Gretzky did with the wrong side of his blade— he'd broken Gordie Howe's record with a backhand and had won game six of the heartbreaking 1993 semifinals in overtime against the Leafs the same way—so he was delighted, but not surprised, having credited Dave Keon for making Gretzky think to use the shot. What made Keon's backhand unique was that he hit the puck hard, almost like a reverse slapshot, sending it screaming at great speeds and at an angle particular to the release. Sometimes he wrenched the puck from the ice like a person trying to dig out the roots of an old tree. Other times he flicked it lightly or scooped it into the air, even slicing at the puck the way a golfer in a sand trap might hack at a hidden ball. He must have scored a hundred goals this way, including one of them on his own team, which he put past Terry Sawchuk in 1967 after winning a faceoff cleanly and with great strength in his own zone.

Slowly moving to centre ice from just inside his blue line, Keon tapped the puck forward, wound in on goalie Michel Plasse, shot, and scored. The Gardens went crazy. The boy would grow up to be a man who would shout and swear at the TV and fist-punch the air when things like this happened, but now the boy just whooped and fell back, tumbling into a joyful ball before being caught in his father's arms sitting on the couch. He tumbled this way twice more during the broadcast, Keon scoring a hat trick after being insulted by his sagging man-boobed owner. Still, the Leafs' backup goalie, Pierre Hamel, couldn't keep the puck out of the net, and the next day Ballard was back at it again, saying that his team had played like "midgets." While the boy had always thought of the owner as a kind of grumpy neighbour or angry old man who smelled like old pants and Vaseline, he'd never seen him as evil. Hating Harold Ballard was a whole new thing.

The boy's week would have been entirely consumed by these feelings had the dadless James Boys not passed on an amazing rumour Friday afternoon that somebody had hidden a stash of *Playboys* in the sewer near the ravine—twenty or so magazines, maybe more. Finding dirty magazines would normally have pushed every other element of the boy's life into the background, but that it happened in a time of Leafs distress made the rumoured discovery even better. Only a moron wouldn't have agreed that looking at naked ladies was a lot better than thinking about fat old Harold Ballard.

The vertical entrance to the sewer was like the mouth of an enormous lamprey, the bars' teeth protecting people from entering the subterranean tunnel. The boys hatched a plan to tell their parents they'd be playing street hockey the next day, not on the road in front of their houses but in the primary school's parking lot, something they

did every now and then. After meeting at the school on
Saturday morning, the boys—Little Johnny and Guido
were there as well as the James Boys, all of them wearing
fat-ribbed ski jackets—walked over to the ravine, where
they tried getting into the sewer. Since the bars were
tight and close together, it fell to Little Johnny to try,
being as small as a terrier with fingers like Peek Freans.
At first, Johnny wasn't sure. He didn't want to grease
his dark brown corduroy pants or ruin his new Cougars,
which he wore despite the cold and snow and which his
parents—recent immigrants from Ukraine—had seen
as a frivolous investment, although one they'd rewarded
Johnny with after he got good marks in math and science.
Walter James—whose "s's" sounded like "th's" because of
two front teeth that stuck out like bent pickets—tried
to goad Johnny into doing it, calling him a chicken and
a wuss and a mo and a dickweed. But Jimmy James—who
spoke normally, even though he was Walter's brother—
took an altogether different tack, telling him what a hero
he'd be if he could secure the bounty, someone everyone
would talk about for years to come after they'd all grown
old and useless.

The boy could tell what Johnny was thinking; how,
in the dark bowels of the sewer, there might be rats and
snakes and ghosts and skeletons and body parts left by
murderers. And spiders; probably spiders. The boy would
never have done it, would never have gone into a strange
dark place void of light and smelling terrible, a nightmarish
landscape of goo and shit and death and danger. Johnny

talked about his shoes and tried to beg out of it, but Jimmy told him, "These magazines are like a great treasure and every great treasure needs a hero to find it. C'mon, Johnny. C'mon."

Johnny stepped sideways toward the bars, and, lucky for him, it looked like he couldn't get in. His shoulders were a little too bony, his legs a little too big. But Jimmy said, "Here, let's help him," and so the boys pressed against Little Johnny with all their weight. While Johnny cried that they were hurting him, the boy pushed a thought out of his head that he stopped himself from sharing: sure, they could help Little Johnny get in, but could they help him get out?

They pushed for a long time, maybe five minutes. Johnny wailed and cried a bit more—sucking back tears so as not to totally destroy the heroic nature of his effort—until, at last, one of his legs popped through. Then another. And then, with a final push, he was in. He stood there looking out like a dog in a kennel.

"What do I do now?" he asked.

"Go! Go!" shouted Walter.

The floor beneath him was wet and muddy and greased with dreck. Little Johnny bent down, took off his shoes, and handed them back through the bars. The boy held them as Johnny disappeared into the tunnel.

The kids vibrated with excitement, and for a while there was silence until Johnny made a sharp cry.

"What'd ya find?" shouted Jimmy, cupping his hands around his mouth.

There was more crying and some sobbing, a forlorn voice echoing through the distance of the long cement chamber.

"My foot! It's bleeding!!"

There was a slushing sound and some more sobbing before Johnny appeared, hopping on one foot with the other crooked at the knee dripping blood. In his hand was a dirty plastic bag weighted with the impossible bounty: five *Playboys*, three *Penthouses*, and one magazine called *Nature's Gift,* a folio of nudist-colony pictures of naked people playing volleyball and croquet. Little Johnny hopped to the bars and passed the bag through, grimacing in pain, his face wet with tears. "Owwwwwwww ..." he said, biting his lip. "It hurts. It really really hurts."

"Let's see," said Jimmy, kneeling down and reaching inside for the bloody foot.

The skin was torn at the heel—probably from broken glass, thought the boy—and Jimmy told Walter, who was staring at the bounty, to remove the magazines and hand over the plastic bag. The boy thought about a word his doctor had once used—"tetanus"—which, he remembered, was a kind of shot that stopped diseases from entering an open wound, or something like that.

"Look at her jugs!!" said Walter, unleafing a centrefold of a woman named Anne Garfield (twenty-three years old; from Wisconsin; loves blueberry pie and ice skating) sitting topless on a red divan holding a bouquet of flowers over her magic parts.

"What about the tetanus?" asked the boy, staring at Anne Garfield as if summoning her to answer.

"Hold your foot here," said Jimmy, tightening the bag around Little Johnny's foot using a shoelace from one of his Cougars. He slid the other sneaker on Johnny's good foot.

"God they're as big as watermelons!" said Guido, his mouth hanging open.

"Shut up!" said Jimmy as Little Johnny shrieked in pain.

"Tetanus," repeated the boy. "You need a doctor for the tetanus!"

Jimmy sealed the bag around Little Johnny's foot and told the guys, "Put down the smut and help me pull."

The boy thought that "smut" was as good a word as "tetanus" in terms of what it stood for. "Smut" meant dirty and gross in a good way while "tetanus" meant something that hurt so something worse wouldn't hurt you. The word "smut" made him excited but the word "tetanus" made him worried. His feelings were confused as he reached behind the bars and grabbed the baby fat of Little Johnny's midsection, trying to yank him to safety. His friend was sweating horribly, soaking the insides of his winter coat.

Little Johnny let himself cry some more, his face damp and pale. After a few minutes his bad foot came through, and after more pulling his body popped out. Jimmy put one of Johnny's arms around his shoulder and told the boys to help before walking him up the side of the ravine. Jimmy said, "Look, Johnny, look at this; look what you got us," pointing to a photo of a cream-skinned brunette with a woolly muff starfished on a rumpled bed, a silver room-service dome sitting near her hip.

Johnny's foot bled in the bag as Walter turned the pages of the magazine. Inside, a dazzling Eden of flesh was revealed: one woman with merry boobs and a Dorothy Hamill haircut riding on horseback across a field; another with a tribble of pubic hair lying poolside while being served a tall drink by a grave and disapproving butler in a dark vest and trousers; another wearing glasses and sitting topless at a desk with a pencil behind her ear, staring in goofy confusion at an open ledger; another with shocking red hair and thimble-sized nipples straddling a hay bale and patting a small white kitten; another dressed as a cheerleader in blond pigtails wearing a red, white, and blue uniform and doing a jump to reveal her smooth, pantyless bum; another brunette wearing a furry-hooded ski jacket zippered halfway up with her boobs peeking out like baby lemurs; another with a bundle of auburn hair tied high on her head emerging naked from the shallow end of a pool, her sand-dollar breasts sparkling after a swim; and one model from *Penthouse*—the magazine that showed things *Playboy* would not—with dark ringlets of hair and long eyelashes who sat looking between her legs, where, using her fingers, she opened a part of herself the boy had never seen before but had heard existed. After Walter turned the last page of the last delicious magazine, the boys sat there stunned before he started over from the beginning.

The day got colder and colder and the sun dipped and so the dadless James Boys stuffed the magazines into their rolled-up winter coats. The boys walked home dazed by what they'd seen, forgetting Little Johnny's orphaned Cougar, which sat like a lonely sentry guarding the dark sewer.

17

Besides all the hockey players who'd come from the region, I was aware of Kirkland Lake because of the federal politician Charlie Angus, whom I'd met back in the late 70s when our respective bands were playing the same small Ontario clubs. The first time I saw Charlie, we'd finished our set and were waiting in the dressing room of Kitchener's Kent Hotel, a strip bar by day and new wave/punk club by night. Charlie's band, L'Étranger—which he'd formed with Andrew Cash, another friend and politician—was supposed to headline the show, but they were late showing up. I was worried about having to play more songs—our band knew only eleven at the time—but while deciding what to do, L'Étranger burst through the door, shaking and drawn. They told us that they'd just finished opening for the Dead Kennedys at the Masonic Temple in Toronto, where they'd been driven from the stage in a hail of spit and blood (there were still bits of mucus on the arms of their leather jackets). Eventually the band took to the stage and they were great. After the show, Charlie told me how much he loved the Canadian north and that one day he might live there. It's what he did a few years later, exiling himself and his family to Cobalt, eight hours north of Toronto. After Charlie got elected to Ottawa he opened a storefront office in Kirkland Lake just down the road from the Hockey Heritage North museum, which the bass player told me I was required to visit should I ever pass through.

Curving out of the teeming countryside, the road cut into town. At the top of the commercial district stood the museum, grey-bricked and modestly built with a huge parking lot that was empty, the town having only just slouched into its low season. Entering the exhibits—but not before reading the guest book, which revealed that Ron Tugnutt, former Nordiques goalie and World Junior assistant coach, had been there a few days before—I discovered that I had the building to myself, save for two men in smudged-dirt baseball caps playing bubble hockey, which they did for the duration of my stay, causing me to wonder whether they were part of the presentation.

Dedicated to hockey in the north, and the players the region produced, the museum was compelling. Unlike Toronto's Hall of Fame—which I'd visited a number of times, both on Bay Street and in its old wooden guise on the grounds of the CNE—it possessed new treasures to tease the eye: an old moth-bitten green and white South

Porcupine sweater; a black and red Abitibi Eskimos jacket; two Maple Leaf Gardens' seats—end blues—signed by Gus Mortson; a black-and-white photo of Phil Esposito as a teenager playing for the Algoma Contractors; and an eight-by-ten of the leather-helmeted 1938 Sudbury Wolves, who'd won the World Championships that year. But it was the Gold Hall—a large, semicircular room with a wide velvet railing holding the gold plaques of its honoured members—that I liked best, filled as it was with names celebrating the area's combustible mix of ethnicities—Beaver Coutu, Réal Chevrefils, Count Grosso, Bep Guidolin, Didier Pitre, Shorty Green, Gerry Toppazzini, Joffre Desilets, Merlyn Phillips, Hillary Menard, Nakina Smith, and Cummy Burton—a wild vowel stew brewed from a spice box of cultures. This was to say nothing of First Nations athletes like Ted Nolan and Chris Simon; Sammy Rothschild, the NHL's first Jewish player; Art Ross, after whom the league's scoring title had been named; and Les Costello, the old Leaf turned Catholic priest turned Flying Father, who was shown mock-wrestling Mike Palmateer in his crease during a charity game from the late 1970s, both players laughing while losing most of their equipment. (Later, I talked to a displaced Rouyn-Norandan named Richard Roy, who remembered Costello spending time in northern Quebec. "The Father helped run the church up there," he told me, "and he was always a gas, a real clown. There was one priest who gave long-winded sermons, and Father Costello, sitting up on the dais, would pretend to snore or fall asleep while all of this was going on. He was also a menace to police, driving his Chevy along the sidewalk and pretty much doing whatever he wanted. He baptized my youngest son, but my brother remembers that he more or less threw some water on him and that was that. When he played hockey he'd give the referee a lot of grief, telling them, 'You can't give me a penalty, I'm a priest! I am a servant of the Lord,' then swearing under his breath all the way to the box.")

I recognized other names in the Gold Hall: Fred Boimistruck, Hector Marini, Walter Tkaczuk, Moe Mantha, Ron Schock, Dale Rolfe, Ab DeMarco, Baz Bastien, Silvio Bettio, Paul DiPietro, and Gene Ubriaco. Other players set my memory alight, like Wayne "Swoop" Carleton from Sudbury, who, after a charity game, told me that my slapshot "couldn't break a pane of glass" (he was right; it couldn't). There was also ex-Penguin Dan Belisle from South Porcupine, whom I'd met while in Newmarket hanging out with the Moncton Golden Flames (Belisle was the team's coach, about whom a recently benched player told me, "He might have played in the NHL. But like I could give a shit"). There was Jim Jones from Espanola, who'd centred Pat Boutette and Jerry Butler on the Leafs' energy line in the late 70s; Jerry "King Kong" Korab from Sault Ste. Marie, who'd once terrorized me as a young writer in the press lounge of the Memorial Auditorium in Buffalo; Dave Tataryn from Sudbury, who played with the Toronto Toros; Ron Francis, also from Sault Ste. Marie, who'd been Keon's roommate in

Hartford but who refused to speak to me for this book; Wilf Paiement from Earlton, who'd once stared at me, spitting gob after gob at his feet, instead of answering a question from me in the dressing room of Maple Leaf Gardens; Toe Blake from Victoria Mines, who'd played against my wife's grandfather in factory baseball leagues; Frank Mahovlich from Schumacher, whom I'd just seen in New York City; and Sheldon Kannegiesser from North Bay, who'd published a book of poetic ballads based on his career called *Warriors of Winter,* which they sold in the museum's gift shop. I bought two copies.

Then there was Bill Barilko. Barilko was northern Ontario's iconic figure, having scored the overtime winning goal for the Leafs in 1951 before disappearing after a plane crash and plunging the team into a decade of championshipless campaigns—a stunning descent in a league of only six franchises. In 1962 his body was found in a swamp near Cochrane, just days after the Leafs won their next Cup, feeding into the mythology that already swirled about the late player. While reading the museum's dedication to him—it was placed next to the familiar photo of the swoop-haired defenceman high in the crease and slapping the puck while T-boning through the air—I couldn't help drawing comparisons between Barilko and Keon, both of whom were from the north and whose absence had affected the Leafs' spiritual fortunes. But if Barilko's fate had been absolute—the result of an unseen hand pulling him from the earth—Keon's disavowment had been self-directed. Both players' effect on the team had been strange and unfortunate, but that the old captain had decided to walk away was stranger still. I harboured a private hope of explaining to Keon that he was giving away something that had been stolen from others, and that, if anything, he should come back to honour those, like Barilko, who couldn't come back themselves. After all, Keon wasn't dead; he was merely living in Florida. I knew there was a joke in there, but I stopped myself as I climbed back into my car and headed east to Rouyn-Noranda.

On the way I decided to stop at Kirkland Lake's Joe Mavrinac Community Complex, which housed a skating rink where seven-foot black-and-white portraits of area players were rumoured to be hanging around the stands. I swerved into the parking lot, raised the collar on my winter coat, and pushed through the cold air toward the centre, which was also home to a swimming pool and gymnasium, and, on this day, handfuls of preteen kids waiting to be picked up from an after-school program.

A few tired-looking mothers sat on benches in the arena's concourse drinking coffee-machine coffee and watching their younger children run around. They eyed me as I moved past them in my fedora, boots, and long coat. I was certain that none of the women wanted to take my picture, nor that they considered me the most interesting man there, although the odds were probably slightly better in Kirkland Lake than in Manhattan. I moved through one door into a hallway, and then another, passing dressing rooms and changing areas. I found

another hallway, another door, and when I pushed it open,
I'd returned to the concourse. The women looked up and
giggled. If I didn't strike them as the most interesting
man, I was certainly the most clueless.

"Um, excuse me?" I said to the mothers, smiling.

"Can I help you with something?" asked one of the
women, crossing her arms and shooting me a look of
broad and exaggerated pity.

Her friend giggled some more.

"The rink," I said, sounding only a little like a doofus.

"YOU want to see the rink?" asked the woman.

"Yes, if I could," I said.

"You know that nobody's playing, right?" said the
other woman.

"Oh, I know," I said. I've come to see the paintings."

The presence of the fancy gentleman finally made
sense to the women. They left their children and escorted
me into the empty rink.

The portraits were just as the people at Hockey
Heritage had promised. Painted by artist Mark Didine,
the canvases were radiant and luminous, running black
and white floor to ceiling around the rink. The two-tone
colour made the subjects appear ghostly, and even more
so in the silence of the clapboard seats that echoed the
once-scraping blades of 60s and 70s star players: the
Plager boys and the Watsons, Mickey and Dick Redmond,
Shakey Walton, and Larry Hillman, who'd played with
Keon in Toronto, and who, after being denied a raise by
Harold Ballard in 1968, predicted that the Leafs would

suffer years of futility until they ponied up the cash, which, of course, they never did. I lingered in front of each canvas, writing down names and numbers, thrilled to have discovered this trove and grateful that I'd stopped by.

Twenty minutes later I walked back through the concourse to find the tired mothers gone. I came out of the rink feeling weary myself—it had already been a long travel day—and with evening looming and my thoughts weighted from all I'd pushed into them, I felt the way one does before sleep: pulled toward the comfort and warmth of rest, even though I still had a forty-minute drive ahead of me. But my calm was shattered by a group of children shouting, the sound of small cries buried inside the noise. I looked past the railing to a patch of grass where a bunch of kids chased another kid. They all wore the same big running shoes and standard-issue nylon jackets humped with Dark Knight or Spider-Man-crested backpacks. I walked toward the children, but as I did my legs buckled and my body grew hot. I felt dizzy and strange the way I had at the Rush concert, and so I bent over for a moment, hands on my knees and fedora brim pointing to the ground. The children shouted and a small voice cried out. I breathed deeply, something I'd been told to do after my first panic attack.

A few moments passed, and by the time I'd straightened up the children had run into the distance of a neighbouring street, big chasing small, as they always had and always would. Once the kids had disappeared my memory tore open and it was all in front of me again:

moment by moment, dream by dream. Suddenly, I knew what it was I had to tell the captain. I had to tell him about Dixon Grove and grade six and Roscoe, whose memory struck me like a paddle to the rib cage. The torn crest and the Flyers. What happened after school. "Seasons in the Sun." Adults who'd watched me being bullied on the grass, and who did nothing. Mrs. Reynolds, her hair, her way. Her voice. Fuzz guitar. My cousins and aunt, who was dead now. My mom, who was gone, too. Cancer. Hot Wheels. Bubblegum. Snow. Peters with the boy boobs. Gandhi. My toqueless head pressed against the grass, then fighting back because the captain had for the first time in his career. The day was April 27, 1975. There was swinging and hitting and falling and more crying. Then relief, goddamned relief. Thirty-eight years ago. It had happened. The thugs. On the corner. I'd talked to them. The sweater. It said KEON. And here I was, going to the captain's hometown. Jesus Christ. I breathed a little easier.

18

1974 passed into 1975. In music, the smooth, bell-bottomed disco of "Kung Fu Fighting" turned into "Why Can't We Be Friends" with its choppy striding rhythm and loud shouting vocals; the slow sweet goo of "The Air That I Breathe" by The Hollies became the strange nervous singing of "Space Oddity," where the astronaut is almost certain he's going to die; "Sundown"—a song that everybody's parents liked—became "At Seventeen," about a girl who is ugly and ignored and which made the boy feel sad in his heart and stomach whenever it came on the radio; and "The Joker" by Steve Miller Band—a funny song where the guitar whistles at the lady—was deposed as the most-played 45 on CFTR by maybe the strangest record ever by a group called Labelle, where four tall black women dressed up in outer-space clothes with missile boobs and crazy pants sang in French about marmalade, of all things, which the boy had tried once and thought was sour, and which John Peters used to bring for lunch every now and then (probably another reason why Roscoe beat him up).

On New Year's Eve, '74, there was a party at the boy's aunt and uncle's place just as there'd been every other New Year's Eve. It was a strange night for the boy because he was mostly left to himself by the adults, who drank beer and champagne and cocktails with ridiculous names and generally behaved the way they didn't every other night of the year. The boy ate chips in the basement and watched a Bruce Lee movie while his parents and relatives carried on at his uncle's stand-up tiki bar, which had a fake straw awning and paintings of almost-nude ladies in grass skirts on the wall. Because he was younger than his two cousins and older than his sister and another cousin, the boy felt disconnected from whatever else was going on. Every now and then his mother came over and asked if he was okay, her breath sour-sweet from the rum cocktails and adult treats, which they called "hors d'oeuvres" and which couldn't have been very tasty seeing as they were French. He told his mom he was fine, then lay across a beanbag chair watching Bruce Lee break some guy's arm. Behind him, the adults shouted and told rude stories he wasn't supposed to hear. Corks popped and glasses clinked. A noisemaker whirled, going *zzzzzzzoiiiiing!* Later on his mom, who wore a flowery blouse and fancy going-out shoes, grabbed him and shouted "Happy New Year!," which seemed like a big deal to everyone in the room but the boy. The reason it wasn't such a big deal was the presents.

Or lack thereof. How a day over the holidays could be considered important without presents was beyond him.

The boy liked staying up late, but he wished he'd gone to bed right after midnight because, pretty soon, a few adults started fighting. It was a real fight, too; not with punching, but with angry shouting and drunken pushing and lots of swearing. The boy saw the whole thing from the start. He was lying across the beanbag when Mr. Rooke—fat-stomached with grotesque hairy arms—nearly fell on him. He could feel the shadow of the man's great weight, and then the crooked toppling of his body, which crashed down in front of the TV and knocked over a table, spilling the boy's mug of Coke. "Whoa, Al!" shouted the boy's father, helping him to his feet. Al's—or rather, Mr. Rooke's—face was like a sinister cartoon the boy had seen of a drunk with X's where his eyes would have been. His uncle handed Mr. Rooke a drink and slapped him on the back. Mr. Rooke nearly tipped over again.

The boy's parents didn't think the boy knew what it meant to be drunk, but he did, having watched shows on TV where there were intoxicated adults, shows like *All in the Family* and *M.A.S.H.* and also *Laugh-In,* which had a character named Foster Brooks who was always hiccuping and slurring his words. Being drunk was usually played for laughs and was kind of absurd and silly, so when Mr. Rooke started yelling at one of the boy's other uncles— Uncle Joe—it showed the boy another way that drinking could affect you, a bad way that he'd never seen on any comedy show before.

Even though he could barely stand up, Mr. Rooke jabbed the boy's uncle in the chest and called him terrible names and used swear words the boy didn't even know existed, words that began with "c" and ended in "nt." Uncle Joe tried to not jab back, but after a while, it was impossible. From what the boy could gather, Mr. Rooke was criticizing his uncle—who was a schoolteacher— for being something called a "self-righteous prick" who "never taught his kids shit." The boy watched from his beanbag chair as his uncle moved at Mr. Rooke, and the boy was pretty sure there was going to be a fight. But the boy's father got between the two men. He told Uncle Joe to calm down. Uncle Vinnie told Mr. Rooke to do the same.

It was the first time the boy had seen his dad act authoritatively among other adults, but even more than that, it actually seemed to work. His dad had somehow made sure that no one hurt each other. He'd acted tough and strong, only as a way of bringing about peace rather than violence. Instead of using strength to start a fight, he'd prevented one. It showed the boy that another role lay between prey and captor, a role where someone used their power for good rather than evil, like Superman or Dave Keon, which in that moment his dad was and would be evermore. He got Mr. Rooke home safely and then came back to the party. There was more drinking and then everybody went home. It was 1975. Before bed, his mom and dad said what a good year it was going to be but how anybody knew that he wasn't sure.

The Leafs, for their part, marked the beginning of the new year by tying the Seals 3–3. The boy read the game reports the next day while lying in his pyjamas in bed. There was nothing in there he didn't already know—Salming had scored a short-handed goal, and both he and Hammarström were the best players on the ice (along with Keon, of course)—but in Milt Dunnell's column, which ran top to bottom at the left of the main story, there was something about Leafs trainer Joe Sgro's hair, a strange topic for sports, thought the boy. "Sgro has had such excellent results from hair transplants that he will go back for more as soon as the season ends," Dunnell wrote. "So far, Joe has had 300 plugs at $10 per pop." The boy had heard of organ transplants before—a French-Canadian kid on the news had been saved after one was flown in on a plane from America—but never a transplant for hair. It seemed like a funny thing to replace, and "300 plugs"—whatever they were—sounded time-consuming and maybe like it would be painful. Besides, it was only hair. You didn't need it to eat or walk around or breathe or anything.

The next game, the Leafs beat the Blackhawks 6–3, and then Detroit 1–0, making winter vacation pretty good in the end, to say nothing of not getting bullied by Roscoe, who was doing God knows what in his time away from school. The winning shut up Harold Ballard for a while, too (the boy imagined Roscoe and Ballard hanging out over the holidays, lying and stealing and doing terrible things to small animals), and gave the Leafs some momentum going into the second half of the season. Doug Favell, the Leafs' backup goalie, played well, winning both games. The team rested Dunc Wilson, who'd played fourteen of fifteen games before Favell's start.

A lot of people had blamed Wilson for the Leafs' inconsistency, but the boy wasn't sure that was fair. In the January 6 edition of *The Globe and Mail,* Dick Beddoes explained a few things about the goalie which the boy had trouble understanding. Wilson told Beddoes, "I know there are some knocks against me ..." after which the columnist listed what those knocks were. Beddoes wrote, "Wilson may have reduced his worth to the Canucks by trifling with dope," a sentence that, to the boy, was like one of those word puzzles next to the comics. "Trifle," like "marmalade," was the name of an awful dessert he'd once tasted at John Peters's birthday party—it was like glue with odd bits of fruit plunged into a swirly clear mass— while a "dope" was someone who was clueless, like Beetle Bailey or Hagar the Horrible. Whatever the meaning, "trifling with dope" had given Wilson a bad reputation, so it mustn't have been good. Beddoes quoted Wilson as saying that "There was also gossip about me being in a speed ring with Dale Tallon and Jim Young of the B.C. Lions. But there's no way you can play goal if you're strung out on speed." To the boy, a speed ring sounded like something good rather than something bad—superheroes were likely to be part of a speed ring; it would help you go faster together, one body whirring the other forward through space—but he knew that being "strung out" was bad, having heard the term before on a new show about cops called *Starsky and Hutch,* which was sort of like *The Odd Couple,* only not funny and with guns and ladies walking around in their underwear. Bad guys on the show were often strung out on drugs, but how this related to speed was impossible to figure. "Speed" couldn't possibly be "drugs" because hockey players didn't do drugs. Besides, "there's no way you can play goal if you're strung out on speed." Like, obviously.

Just after New Year's another new show about being strung out and other things started on TV, a show that was just a person's name: *Barney Miller.* At first the boy wondered why anyone would watch something with such a lame name about lame subjects like being strung out before he realized that the show was a comedy. Looking back after the boy became a man, he recognized the show as groundbreaking in this regard: taking serious subjects and using them as the raw matter for comedy, which was actually black comedy, a term that hadn't been invented yet, or if it had, wasn't yet popular.

The show took place in a cop shop. All the characters had unpleasant faces and strange names ("Fish" and "Wojo" and "Luger" and "Ripner") and most of them were depressed and always pushing each other's buttons, if in a way that was weary and self-hating, although, to the boy, they mostly just seemed angry. Every show, the cops had to deal with types of people the boy never knew existed: men who showed their weiners to people on subways, bombers who blew up buildings, prostitutes, neighbourhood vigilantes, pimps, social workers, group-home kids, people who jumped off bridges, conspiracy theorists, juvenile pickpockets, men who liked to wear lingerie, kleptomaniacs, number-runners, sperm-bank clerks, pornographers, religious cultists, and drug addicts. In fact, it was after one new episode called "You Dirty Rats" that the boy learned that "dope" was another word for "drugs," which probably explained why Dunc Wilson was such a lousy goalie.

The head of the police crew was Barney Miller. He was always shaking his head and wiping his brow and hiding his face in his hands because the people he arrested created a great disturbance for him. Life in the cop shop—it was called a "precinct"—was a freak show compared to what the boy knew living in the suburbs. There were hostage takings, shootings, ODs (what happened when you got too strung out), accidental jail-cell births, and sometimes assault and killing. Because *Barney Miller* was broadcast in prime time, the boy would watch it and then go to bed. Sometimes he'd lie between the sheets thinking about what had happened and what he'd seen and whether people actually showed their shwangs to other people in public. One episode was called "The Child Stealers," where, according to the TV guide, "Barney has his hands full with a self-proclaimed time traveller and a divorced father who tries to kidnap his son." The boy stayed up late thinking about the episode, how heartbroken the son was because his parents fought all the time, hoping against hope that they'd get back together. To a list that included "Must Go to Heaven" and "Get Married" and "Don't Steal" he quickly added "Don't Ever Get Divorced," because in this episode it looked like a terrible thing. Even the officers ended up learning a lesson from the boy and his parents: that, no matter how much grief they got from their wives or girlfriends—they groused about this kind of thing all the time—love in any form was okay, and, well, at least they weren't running around kidnapping their own children. Sometimes the boy wondered if Roscoe's parents were like the ones in "The Child Stealers." Maybe they were confused and depressed, like the kidnapping dad on the show. Maybe they fought all the time, which the boy's parents did once in a blue moon, their voices raging like cannon fire down the hallway. Even though he hated the bully—he hated him from the tip of his fingers to his big toes, which, at eleven years old, weren't big at all—the thought of Roscoe lying in his bed in the dark with pillows covering his face as his parents yelled and screamed actually made the boy feel sad. It was absurd, but there it was. The boy clicked off the lamp on his bedside table, then dreamed he was falling. No one was there to catch him.

19

I rolled into Rouyn-Noranda just after dusk, the lights of DEPOT EROTIQUE and SALON CHEVEAUX AUX VENTS and TAVERN LES SPORTIF and PHARMAPRIX and BINGO DU CUIVRE and VACHON SPORTS allowing me the shiver of suddenly feeling like I was in a new place. Men in long coats and women in tall boots moved along the sidewalk, their arms looped at the elbow, passing candlelit restaurants and bars just beginning to thrum. The town was small but lively and people seemed to move about with a purpose, as opposed to the straggling few I'd noticed on the streets of Kirkland Lake and Timmins, which, I suppose, had their own kind of rugged charm. Later on, I suggested this to my server at the elegant restaurant in my hotel— Le Cellier—who turned her head as if smelling a bad smell. "Kirkland? Charming?" she said, her Gallic accent giving the response an exaggerated sense of outrage.

Once I'd checked into the hotel, I secured a café au lait from Le Saint-Exupéry bistro, the frothy drink warming my hands in its cup as I walked down Perrault Avenue to Centre d'exposition de Rouyn-Noranda, where a man named Yvon Martin waited for me on its steps dressed in a sport jacket and pressed trousers and smoking a long white cigarette. Yvon was the brother of former Wing, Bruin, and Blackhawk Pit Martin, who'd died in a tragic snowmobile accident a few years earlier. The elder Martin spoke fine English—"I never studied, I just learned from the neighbours," he said—and was a walking hockey encyclopedia in fine shoes and cologne. His life, and his playing career—mostly intermediate or senior, as well as amateur—had intersected with almost every important figure from Rouyn-Noranda. For a while in the 1960s he coached the Noranda Copper Kings, and one fall an elfin goalie with long arms from nearby Palmarolle showed up to try to win a spot in the crease. "I've done a few things in hockey," said Yvon, "and one of them was hiring Rogatien Vachon. But I also fired him. We had three other goalies in camp, including Louis Levasseur, who became the Leafs' practice goalie, and Ted Ouimet, who played for the Blues. We had a weak team and the goalies saw eighty shots a night. We were losing a lot and I had to make a change. Still, I think you could say it was a bad call," he said, shrugging his shoulders.

Yvon was Dave Keon's neighbour growing up on Murdoch Street. "After the war, people came to Rouyn-Noranda from all over the world," Yvon told me as we walked into the museum. "There were Italians, Irish, Greeks, and Jews, and the Eastern Europeans—Poles, Ukrainians, and Russians—liked it because they'd worked in the mines back home. And of course there were the English and the French. I suppose there was some fighting, but not as much as you'd expect. People talk about big cities like Montreal and Toronto having this particular ethnic mix, but we were no different; it's just that we were remote, far away from everything. In the 40s and 50s it was a thriving place and hockey was at the centre of that. For a town of thirty-five thousand, we ranked third in the province after only Montreal and Quebec City for players sent to the NHL. Not bad, wouldn't you say?"

"Not bad at all," I said, nodding.

For a long time, the only rink in town was in Noranda (the two cities were separate until amalgamation in 1970), which was fine except for the fact that most of the people lived in Rouyn, a jumble of small homes and businesses located a good distance from the mines. "Rouyn was where the action was, and people lived here because it was away from the mines," Yvon told me. "There were twenty hotels, countless clubs and bars, lots of nightlife. Kids played hockey outside on Lake Osisko and on frozen school lots. The place where we're standing right now"—he pointed to the floor of the gallery entrance—"was an old school called St. Michael's. It's where we played hockey. Just two lights, one at either end."

"You played here?" I asked him.

"Sure I did."

"And Keon? He played here?"

"Of course."

"Right here?"

"Yes, right here."

I looked at my feet.

"Fifty years ago, there was lots of outdoor skating," Yvon continued. "In 1933/34, Noranda Mines built a covered arena with natural ice and room for about twelve hundred people. All the teams played there until 1949, when Rouyn built the Forum, which is across the street from here. Noranda then built the Noranda Recreational Centre—now Arena Dave Keon—with the help of miners during their off-hours. It's still the oldest rink in the QMJHL—also the smallest—and remains the focus of the city."

Of the Recreational Centre, Jim Keon later said, "There are three things that make a good athletic program, and the first is a great facility (the other two are coaching and a role model for younger players to follow; that was my brother). The building was enormous for its time—two hundred by eighty-five feet—and had two thousand seats, a rifle range, a gymnasium, and dance studios. It gave intermediate and senior hockey a place to develop, and because the mine was such a large and steady employer, lots of great former junior players skated there. Some very famous games were played by skaters who, while they might not have made the six-team NHL, showed the younger generation—including my brother—what intensity and commitment to the sport was all about."

Back in the day, the Centre also hosted concerts. The Everly Brothers played there on the day "Bye Bye Love" went to number one, their breakout moment in rock and roll. "I remember where I was sitting," Yvon said, "and how excited the band was. It was a big day in music, a historic day. And it happened in our city," he told me, pulling at his sleeves and looking proud.

"Between the Centre and the Radio Hotel (Rouyn-Noranda's legendary nightspot) there was always music in town," Jim told me. "The Hawks used to play in the lounge, and The Stampeders once had their equipment stolen and had to buy it back from thieves before they could play. Because of the sunset law (at dusk, mega-radio stations in the U.S. were allowed to boost their wattage, sending their signals clean across the relatively flat Canadian north), kids of my generation grew up on WGR from Buffalo, WLS from Chicago, WABC in New York, WOWO in Fort Wayne, Indiana. Through them I heard things I'd never heard before, and, to be honest, it fed my desire to see things beyond the north, giving me a sense of wanderlust and ultimately making my decision to leave a lot easier. I was fourteen years old in October, 1960, when me and a friend, Mike Roche, decided to hitchhike to Toronto. We told our parents that we were going to somebody's cottage for the long weekend. We eventually got to Toronto and stayed at the west-end Y on College Street. We showed up at the Gardens and talked the usher into letting us in. It was my brother's first time playing at home with the Leafs, but coming off the ice, he hardly even looked at me. He just said, 'Does Mom know you're here?' I was so awestruck by the city that his teammate Ron Stewart said, 'If you keep looking up, you're going to get sunburn on the roof of your mouth.' The next day, Jim Gregory picked us up at the Y and drove us out on the 400 highway. It was a great time and I'll remember it for as long as I live."

I asked both men about a story I'd read in Bobby Baun's book in which the Leafs defenceman talked about coming to the north in the late 1950s during the Leafs' pre-season, where they trained a little, put on an exhibition for local fans, and watched some juvenile hockey. Baun described how nervous Dave Keon was about skating in front of his future teammates and how his mother had to talk him out of quitting hockey after the game. He also wrote about how, in the evenings, the team would go to the Radio Hotel to watch Stompin' Tom Connors perform. The timeline didn't make sense to me—Tom hadn't started touring until the 1960s—but Yvon said, "In Rouyn-Noranda, he wasn't a proper musician. He worked in the mines like everyone else and played a little on the side. He wasn't Stompin' Tom Connors, not yet. He would have come here for work like the others did." Remembering Tom's song "Movin' On to Rouyn" and the words "I'm a honkytonk player just drifting along," the clouds lifted from Yvon's theory. I told him that I thought there must have been few things better than the Maple Leafs of the late 1950s sitting around drinking and watching Tom Connors play in a tavern in northern Quebec.

After touring the museum's small yet beautifully curated exhibit—"Rouyn-Noranda: Monde du Hockey"— Yvon drove me to Murdoch Street past the old Keon home. The family had originally come from the Ottawa Valley with other Scottish and Irish to work in the mines, many of them settling in a cluster on this same strip of road. I was half-expecting the house to radiate as if a profound force were supporting it from deep inside the earth, but the bungalow sat still and white on its modest lot, just like the others on the street. Still, I told myself that it was across this lawn and down this street that the captain as a boy had run to the rinks of the city, leaving his mother stooped in the small door frame of their home shouting at him to be careful.

By all accounts, Mrs. Keon—it's what everyone called her—was a mighty figure in Rouyn-Noranda as well as a towering presence in the captain's young life. She came by her love of hockey honestly, having been related to 40s Maple Leafs star Tod Sloan, born in Vinton, Quebec, near Gatineau and the Ottawa Valley. Keon's mom rarely ceded responsibility to his father (nicknamed "Shorty"), whom she'd met in Duparquet. Mr. Keon was forty-nine at the time—a lifetime bachelor—and together they had eight children, losing two to unfortunate pregnancies. Dave's father was quieter and more resolute in how he went about his life; Jim remembered him as "a typical miner and great guy who worked hard and paid the bills but found little time for leisure. I don't think he ever skated once in his life."

"I don't think a lot of people knew David's father very well," said Richard Roy, who was an old friend of the Keon family, "but Mrs. Keon was a very charming woman. She always took in billets, so Dave was around hockey players from a very early age." (She continued to do this after her son made the NHL, once billeting former Toro star Wayne Dillon for a tournament.) "Mrs. Keon treated everyone with care and respect. She was a devout Catholic, too, and instilled a lot of those beliefs in her kids, which is why it was important for her to see Dave go to St. Michael's College in Toronto [home of the Leafs' junior team]." It was the promise of an education among the brothers at St. Mike's that favoured the Leafs' chances of signing Keon to a C-Form contract. The Leafs also hastened to sponsor Keon's midget club as a way of currying favour with Mom and Dad, but especially Mom. I was told that at games Mr. Keon would sit quietly in the stands, a set of rosary beads in his hands, murmuring a prayer under his breath. "He was very quiet at the games," said Jim. "I think he was uneasy there. Once, someone in the crowd shouted at my brother to hustle, or something like that, and it bristled with my dad."

Yvon and I drove through an old part of the city, down wide looping streets once crooked with miners' tenements but long since divided into proper homes. "There was a Russian Orthodox church here," he said, pointing out the window, "and a synagogue there. Growing up, there were six movie theatres and twenty-nine hotels. Action: all the time," he told me. Later

I called Saul Korman, who grew up in the city, to get what I thought would be an opposing impression of the preposterously utopian nature of Rouyn-Noranda in the 50s and 60s, but he agreed with Yvon. "The Jews would get together to play poker and the Arab guys would join in," he said. "A war could have been happening between them in one part of the world, but you wouldn't have known it in Rouyn-Noranda." It made me wonder whether the city's harmony and relative peace had affected the captain's manner on the ice. If northern Alberta produced scrappers and pugilists, R-N had yielded gentle, if hard-nosed, skaters, from Keon to Houle to Lapierrière to Pit Martin to Dale Tallon to the Turgeons, not a goon among them. Proposing this theory to Jim, he paused and considered. "I hadn't thought of that before. But back then, everyone seemed to find a way to get along despite the differences."

We drove back to the museum, then Yvon pointed across the street. "There," he said, gesturing to a long grey building, "is the Rouyn Forum, named for Jacques Lapierrière and Réjean Houle, two more great products of hockey here, especially Houle, who always comes back to visit. The rink was partly rebuilt and another surface was added to the main pad, but it's the same inside as it's been for forty years. I'll let you visit it on your own because I have to tend to a few things," he said, "but when you're walking around, remember this: hockey in Rouyn-Noranda never would have become what it is were it not for one man."

"Yes, I know," I said. "Dave Keon."

"Well, him as well," laughed Yvon. "But there was someone who taught the men who also taught Dave Keon. And that man was Wilf Cude."

I swallowed my breath. "Wilf Cude?" I said, wanting to hear the name voiced once again in the cold evening air.

"Yes, Wilf Cude. James Murdoch brought him in here to organize things, to bring Rouyn-Noranda together and to build the hockey program. He helped teach Vince Thompson and Stan Tallon, and those were the men who taught Dave Keon. If it weren't for Wilf Cude, all of this might never have existed."

I shook my head. Not only was "Wilf Cude" the kind of hockey name you didn't often come across—like Peanuts O'Flaherty, Wren Blair, Ching Johnson, or Shrimp Worters, it evoked a wartime comic strip or a silent film featuring villains in capes and heroes in scarves and felt hats—but the 1930s Red Wing goaltender was also one of the figurative hooks on which much of my creative life had developed. I'd first come across his name in Melville, Saskatchewan, during one of my band's early tours. We'd named our second record after the town—it was the name of our pedal steel guitar player, too—and before our show at the Waverly Hotel, the mayor made us honorary citizens, presenting us with scrolls on the postage-stamp stage in the corner of the room. Earlier in the day I'd stood in the dark concourse of the town's wood-ribbed rink and written down a list of former Melville Millionaire players: Eddie Shore, Sid Abel, John

Ferguson, Duane Rupp, Brian Propp, Ron Hextall, Kelly Buchberger, as well as Wilf Cude. I later sought out further information about the team's alumni, but I'd always stop at Cude, since so little was known about his life. The one thing I did learn was that he'd been discovered playing in the very same building by scout Frank Fredrickson, the dashing Manitoban violinist who'd also won a gold medal as a member of the Winnipeg Falcons.

The first time I was ever asked to contribute to a book—*Original Six,* edited by my late friend Paul Quarrington—I researched the story of Cude facing Charlie Gardiner during the 1933 Detroit–Chicago Stanley Cup final. Cude was a Welshman and Gardiner a Scot, and in the deciding game they duelled each other 0–0 through five periods before thimble-sized Harold "Mush" March won for the Hawks in triple overtime. Gardiner had been suffering blackouts prior to the final—a fact he'd kept hidden from team doctors—and on the day of the last game he awoke cursed by blindness before his sight returned to him at midday. In the dressing room before the match, he told his teammates that all he needed to win was one goal—which, in the end, took the Hawks 120 minutes to secure. The next day he was taken around the Loop in a wheelbarrow after winning a bet with another player. I told the story from Gardiner's perspective, but Cude was the keyhole through which I passed into my first significant work.

A few years later I was playing shinny at McCormick Arena in Toronto. After the game one of the goaltenders asked me about my story in *Original Six,* then told me that he was dating Wilf's granddaughter. I peppered him with questions about the old goalie, but he threw up his hands, telling me that his girlfriend knew no more about her grandfather than anyone else. It became an obsession of mine to find out as much as I could about him. When I revealed this to Yvon, he nodded his head and confessed, "This is also my obsession," his hands warming in his blazer pockets as snow fell lightly from the grey-blue sky.

Born in Barry, Wales, near Vale of Glamorgan, Cude was the smallest goalie to ever play in the league, standing just over five-eight. He wore a tweed cap and spoke in paradiddles, his tongue moving like a drumstick to a snare, rattling off thoughts at breakneck speed. Cude dealt largely in volume, a jabberjaw who spoke a parochial southern Welsh voiced with prairie patois, which he acquired by way of his adopted city, Winnipeg, home to so many other goaltending legends, including his mythic opposite, Charlie Gardiner. Every now and then Cude would skate from his crease during a break, fetch a pen and paper that he kept on his team's bench, and write a note to the referee or an opposing player, most of them complimentary or heartfelt. At the beginning of his career he had the best and worst job in hockey: travelling around Canada and the American northeast filling in for NHL teams whenever their regular goalies were injured. He kept a wardrobe of six sweaters and matching socks, journeying by Pullman from rink to rink wherever he was needed. A league-wide substitute, Cude was forced to get along with his fellow players, since he'd be playing with them in one game, against them in the next. Cude was cherished by many but loved by few. Fans could only get so close to the goalie; they knew he'd be gone as soon as he arrived. Wilf flirted with hearts, only to carry his love elsewhere.

Owing to his success in Detroit, the Canadiens put him on their permanent roster. Cude was thrilled at the chance to play full-time for a single club and pitched a shutout every third game, but in the end he backstopped the Habs in their least successful epoch, giving way to the crosstown Maroons, Stanley Cup winners in 34/35. Meanwhile the Welshman took command of a Shell service station across the street from the Montreal Forum, and despite the team's struggles, he continued to work on the elements of his position. In the summertime he built a makeshift net in his backyard where, dressed in full equipment, he'd invite neighbours and their children to shoot tennis balls and sponge pucks at him for hours in the blazing sun. Cude showed up at training camp in equipment streaked with grass stains and greased with sweat. The Canadiens offered to pay for a new set of equipment, but he refused. The same applied to team sweaters: no matter how torn or faded, the Welshman wore the same puck-bitten rags his entire career, loath to corrupt whatever forces had conspired to get him to the big time.

He was also a slave to superstition. According to writer Andrew Podnieks, Cude "played with a rabbit's foot stuffed into the top of one of his pads. Before every game he wedged it in, and after every game he took it out." The March 29, 1945, edition of the *Toronto Star* told the story of how, "when he played for the Canadiens, Cude's wife would drive him to the rink, only to stop the car a half mile away, where the goalie would walk the rest of the way to get the benefit of the wintry breezes. If the team won, she'd stop in the same spot the next game. If they lost, Wilf picked a new place." In the same column the writer told the story about the day Cude decided to quit hockey, a tale famously recorded in Randall Maggs's stupendous and beautiful book *Night Work*, about Terry Sawchuk. According to legend, Wilf and his wife were eating his game-day meal at home—steak and a loaf of bread—when the table legs squeaked once, then again, from the force of Wilf's slashing cutlery. At this point in his career Cude had gathered countless miles under him, having toiled for every league franchise (including the old Philadelphia Quakers, whose single 1930/31 NHL season set the league record for futility with a .131 winning percentage, a mark later broken by Washington in 1974/75). Over time, Cude had stopped writing notes. His nerves had feathered, his thoughts had been clouded by self-doubt, and he'd fallen silent. He'd started to play to his size, and after a while teams went into the stands for a substitute goalie rather than pay the Welshman's train fare.

As Cude sawed at his meat the table squeaked a third time, and something in the small goalie snapped. He grabbed the meat with two hands and threw it, ketchup-splattered, across the room. The steak hit the wall, SPLAP!, and held there. Wilf gathered his thoughts and solemnly told his wife, "If that steak comes down, I'm finished with this game." The meat dragged slow and heavy down the wall to the hardwood floor, ending Cude's career.

He retired to work at the service station with the best goals against average in the league—he remains number seven on the all-time list—but in the end he spent very little time at the garage. He did a little coaching for the Montreal Junior Canadiens, where he hired Sam Pollock, the future Hall of Fame GM, as his stick boy. In 1946 he was hired to scout for both Montreal and Detroit and continued to travel wherever he was needed, seeing this skater in northern Michigan, that one in The Pas. Whereas some retired players found their post-career wanting, Cude carried himself as if freed from the barrel. To him, the taste of the game was just fine from the stands.

He settled in Rouyn-Noranda at the behest of James Murdoch, who secured him employment as a local Imperial Oil rep. Cude founded the Toilers (a juvenile team named for a Winnipeg basketball club killed in a tragic bus crash), later signing Serge Savard, who'd come to Rouyn-Noranda for school, to the Red Wings. A few years after that the young defenceman went to Cude and begged him to talk James Adams into releasing him to the Habs. Such was the respect and admiration that Adams—a notoriously hard man—had for Cude that he released the future Hall of Famer at the goaltender's insistence.

"That's what Cude was like," said Yvon. "He had a gruff exterior, but also a heart of gold." As Jim Keon remembered him, Cude was "a nervous little guy, always smoking two cigarettes at once, but he was an entrepreneur and a self-made man. He coached me a few times, and I remember him telling me, 'Don't forget to just take the puck and go every now and then. You're not going to develop just playing in a system,' which, when you think about it, is sort of the opposite advice that coaches give kids these days."

Jim also told me that, before his brother signed with the Leafs, Wilf brought him by bus to Hamilton in an attempt to get him to sign with the Red Wings. "I remember David calling home and talking to our mother, telling her that he wanted to sign with Detroit. But my mother would have none of it. He was going to St. Mike's or he was going nowhere. Wilf accepted her decision and that was that. He honoured her views, because that's the kind of person he was."

"One season," Yvon recalled, "my dad and my brothers and I went down to Toronto, to Maple Leaf Gardens. We arrived on Saturday night planning to go to the Sunday matinee—Marlies versus Peterborough, followed by St. Mike's versus Hamilton—where five or six kids from our neighbourhood were playing. The Leafs were facing Detroit on Saturday, so we met Wilf at the Royal York Hotel. We were standing there in the lobby when, all of a sudden, Conn Smythe and Jack Adams came through and saw him. They went bananas and gave him a great reception. It was important to see Wilf in this context, to see the respect and credibility he had. I remember Smythe asking him, 'Hey, Wilf, you ready to go tonight?' Wilf looked at him and said, 'I'd play in bare feet if I had to.'"

After that story Yvon said he was late for his appointment, and disappeared in his sleek black car. I continued thinking of Wilf Cude as I walked into the Houle-Lapierrière arena, which, at first blush, seemed like a good place for hockey ghosts: it was dark and cold, with painted concrete stairs and a stand of old red, blue, and gold benches that squeaked when you pushed them down. A series of banners hung over the ice honouring those who'd played for the midget double A Citadelles, formed in 1964. The names on the flags furthered the story of hockey in northern Quebec: Pierre and Sylvain Turgeon, Stéphane Matteau, Gina Kingsbury, Éric Desjardins, Jacques Cloutier, Richard Lemieux, André Racicot, and, incongruously, former Leaf Gord McCrae, who, while suffering through a short, disappointing career with Toronto, helped the midget Citadelles become the first Quebec team to win the northern Ontario championship in 1964, an event still heralded and discussed among local sportocrats.

Later in the day I met Gilles Lapierrière himself, the paterfamilias of local hockey for whom the junior A Huskies' pink tiger mascot, "Lappy," was named. Gilles told me how he'd talked McCrae back into playing after the goaltender had quit the game, racked by the pressures of expectation. "In late 1963 I went to old man McCrae," Lappy said in the hallway of the Huskies' rink, "and asked if I could talk to his son. He told me that Gord had no skates, and so I said I'd buy him a pair, and that if things went well he could pay me back at the end of the year. In the first game we ended up beating Kirkland Lake

8–5, and as we came down the hallway afterward, the old man stood at the bottom of the stairs smiling and waving around a cheque in his hands." Lapierrière spoke English through a thick French accent, and after a while I recognized these duelling linguistic cousins—one language traded for the other inside single conversations like black and red licorice—as the sound of the city.

In the rink's concourse stood a tall, finger-smudged trophy case with signed sweaters, photos, and old cardboard hockey cards bowed after years sitting on the shelves. There was also Dave Keon's pale wooden stick, which tilted in melancholy against the glass. I put my nose up to the case hoping to establish an immediate— if admittedly sociopathic—intimacy with the Sherwood, while players in full equipment—the young 2012 Citadelles—filed behind me on their way to the practice surface attached to the main pad. I studied the blade, taped black and milled straight—one of Keon's hallmarks that served his famous backhand—the mere sight of it making me ever hopeful about getting closer to my hero. The young players probably asked themselves what the man in the hat and long coat was doing with his face against the wardrobe, but I didn't care. I wanted to smash the glass and grab the stick. I wanted to lean over it and pretend I was angled in concentration at the faceoff circle. I wanted to feel its rare power if only until handcuffed and dragged to the Rouyn-Noranda jail.

Coming out of the rink, I continued on foot through the evening to the Arena Dave Keon, a square building with a glowing fluorescent maw, eyeline to the road, into which people entered for the evening's game: Rouyn-Noranda versus Baie Comeau. It was here that the fourteen-year-old Keon was coached and discovered by Vince Thompson, although Yvon Martin insists that it was Wilf Cude who saw Keon first. Thompson's discovery made him an official Leafs scout after years of bird-dogging for the club, and his team, the Noranda Lions, was infused with four thousand dollars of Conn Smythe's sponsorship cash, a king's ransom in those days to secure a single player. Keon's destiny was shaped in this rink, and so was the end of his childhood. Here began his life as a man and a legend.

On the street, more and more cars blinked through nightfall. Hands pressed in my pockets, I thought of my own life from boy to man, counting the events of 1974/75 as if gathering pieces of a cracked fresco unswept on the cold floor of memory. I thought of the bully Roscoe, and the code by which I'd carried myself through my young life. I thought about how the captain's qualities—leadership, honour, fairness, toughness—had affected me, trying not to shake my head at the naïveté with which I'd put so much faith in one player—one man—whom I'd never met. As a boy, I'd believed that I could build a life using Keon's principles, and an afterlife, too, because believing in God and Love and Heaven and being a good person had once been as important to me as anything else. I tried measuring what percentage of these old tenets remained despite having been tested by Roscoe's beatings, the Leafs' sorry legacy, and the passing of time and age. Still, if I felt burdened by the past—or rather by the attempt to quantify its effect—I told myself that I hadn't let it crush me. After all, I was in Quebec, in Keon's birthplace. I was on the road and moving. Everything I believed in was still alive.

Before heading into the rink, I stood for a moment longer in the glow of the arena lights, the captain's name written in gold letters above me. I could hear the murmuring of the crowd inside, the distant thump of the pregame music, and the jangle of cash registers being opened and closed. Just then, an idea took hold. I hadn't thought of it before, but in an instant it seemed obvious to me: Dave Keon wasn't the only person from my past I had to find.

20

At school, the boy knew kids from pretty much every part of the world. There were Polish kids, Ukrainian kids, Greek kids, Portuguese kids, Italian kids, and Asian kids. There were African kids, too, although he didn't know this at first. One day at the end of school, a brown-skinned girl two lockers over wearing Coke-bottle glasses with dark curls bundled tight to her head tsked after the boy threw his books defeatedly into the bottom of their cell, telling him that he made too much noise. Exasperated and angry with his life and Roscoe and the Leafs—they'd played terribly and had lost 3–1 to Washington the night before—the boy used a word he'd only ever used once in his life and would never use again. He called the girl a "Paki." Then he told her to shut up.

"Paki" was a word as common to the suburbs as "hatchback" or "asphalt" or "Argos" or "Molson's." Over a handful of years, refugees from Bangladesh, Pakistan, and other countries that the boy wasn't even sure were actual places had come to the neighbourhood, settling ten to a family in some of the area's surrounding high rises, one of them even dubbed "Paki Palace." If you stood long enough in one place outside the Smoke and Gift or drugstore or A&P, you'd inevitably hear people complaining about how the Pakis smelled or dressed or talked, although his parents never spoke about this at home, which isn't to say they didn't reflect on it. The boy had wandered outside once when his parents were sitting on lawn chairs between the houses talking with their neighbours, an older couple named Martha and Pete, who were kindly and always forthcoming with sweets, chips, and pop. The boy played with his action figures in the tall grass while the adults kept talking, certain that the boy's mind was preoccupied, which, of course, it wasn't, even when he appeared lost in space. Pete—a train conductor who worked for CN—asked the boy's parents, "If David wanted to marry a black girl, what would you do?" The boy's father paused. "If he loves the girl," he said, "it doesn't matter who he marries." The boy was too young to measure the weight of what he'd said, but he knew there was something different about the way his father had said it: resolved and serious, defiant even. This stayed with the boy as he grew to be a teenager and then a man and then an older man. The only thing that mattered was love. The idea sounded pretty important.

After the boy had called his schoolmate a "Paki"—he'd said it as if spitting out a gross candy—the brown-skinned girl told him, "I'm not a 'Paki.'" The boy said she was lying, but the girl was adamant. "I'm not a 'Paki.' I'm from Africa."

This confused the boy, but it ended up being true: the girl was from someplace in Africa named either Mozambique or Mombasa or Uganda (to him, these names all sounded the same). Maybe one day the boy and the girl from Africa would fall in love and get married, and while this notion made him shake his head like a person trying to dislodge a stuck coin out of a toy bank, since his dad had said it, maybe it would come true. The girl stood at her locker waiting for the boy to say something, and finally he did. He told the girl he was sorry. It felt good because it wasn't like saying sorry for breaking a plate at home or yelling at his sister or staying up with his light on after his parents had told him to go to bed. It was an apology that he'd volunteered. It made him feel a little older, a little more like a man or a real person. Then he walked outside to the grass in front of the school, where Roscoe punched him and said terrible things about the Leafs' loss to Washington until the bully's arms grew too tired to care.

Of all the denominations represented at the boy's school, the only obvious omission were those who spoke French and came from Quebec, which, the boy learned, was Canada's second biggest province. The boy was glad no one in his school spoke French because he hated French class more than any other. The words were even worse than Italian, which he had to speak only once a week at his nonna's on Sundays, while French class happened every day. Certain words—especially "r" words like "voiture" and "chambre" and "écrire"—made him sound as if he was clearing gunk out of his throat, an ugly sound, uglier because they were difficult to say. If math made his brain hurt and gym made his legs sore and geography filled his head with ridiculous names for stupid rock formations and lakes nobody cared about, French class gave him a tender throat and a tired tongue. At the beginning of the year the teacher had made a long, boring speech about how Canada was founded and why it was important to know French in case any of the kids grew up to travel the country, but the boy thought the idea was silly, because other than Florida he had no desire to go anywhere. The teacher worked out of a language book featuring two cartoon figures named George and Xavier who wore little scarves with fancy hair and gaylord clothes. There was no way the boy would ever meet anyone like them and why he had to learn their dumb language he didn't know.

One other thing factored into his unflagging dislike of the French language, French class, and the French people of Quebec, and that thing was the Montreal Canadiens. The boy hated the Canadiens for the same reason everyone else on his street did: they were the Leafs' rivals, and ever since the boy had been watching hockey, the Canadiens—called "the Habs" by French people—almost always beat the Leafs. The boy hated the Habs players. He hated Larry Robinson and his big red moustache and how he ended up winning Norris trophies that Börje Salming should have won. He hated Jacques Lemaire and his stupid helmet and he hated Yvan Cournoyer and how his tongue used to fall out of his mouth whenever he skated fast. He hated Guy Lapointe's long nose and hair pasted flat to his head and he hated Peter Mahovlich for how tall he was and he hated Bob Gainey because he always seemed to be so excited skating down the ice. He hated Henri Richard because he was old and he hated Jim Roberts because he was ugly. He hated it whenever the team brought out people like Jean Béliveau or Maurice Richard or Aurèle Joliat to drop the puck before games and he hated how the anthem singer always looked as if he were about to explode, his pyramid of white hair shaking like a frothing, snow-peaked volcano. If the Montreal Forum—he hated that, too—had been hit by a comet or space junk or a Russian missile, he wouldn't have cared. Montreal was stupid and so was French, which is the language everyone spoke while watching the Habs play. And now his teachers were making him learn it.

The boy hated Ken Dryden, but a little less so. Since Ken and his brother, Dave, had grown up in Etobicoke, they were often around in the summertime, hanging out at the ball diamonds and tennis courts of the new suburb. Both were tall and gentle men, and seeing Ken out of his sweater was like seeing someone altogether different, not so much a player as a person or a man. One year the boy played on a softball team at Martingrove Flats, and for a few games Dave came out to help coach the team. The boy was suspicious of Dave because he was Ken's brother, and being a member of the Sabres didn't help, although he hated them less than the Habs. The boy was an excellent softball player—he could hit, he could field, and he could run—so Dryden spent most of his time with the other players, which was fine with the boy. After one game someone produced a football, and the players ran for passes thrown to them in the outfield by the boy, who was good at football, too. After a few passes, Dryden loped across the grass and yelled to him, "Hit me!" Because the Sabres goalie was so tall, he proved an entirely new target for the boy, who flung the ball with the full extent of his power and ability. It sailed in a perfect spiral and, impossibly, hit the goaltender right between the letters, which is what he said after he'd caught the pass: "Right between the letters!" Walking toward the boy and cradling the ball like a small plump hen, he told him that he was pretty sure he could make the CFL if he worked hard and kept on playing. The boy wanted to tell the goalie that he'd never played organized football before, but didn't. Something about that moment showed the boy that hockey people were mostly good people no matter who they played for, because, even though Dryden had no connection to the Maple Leafs, he'd made him feel pretty good about himself. For a moment, it didn't feel weird being around someone whose job it was to beat the Maple Leafs, which was weird in itself.

Other than the Canadiens players, the boy didn't like Montreal's announcers either. Their names were Dick Irvin and Danny Gallivan and they had nattering voices and big hiccuping accents. Even though the boy would grow up to be a man who would learn that Gallivan's accent came from the Maritimes—PEI—instead of French Canada, it didn't matter. Because he called Habs games he was a Hab, and that made him the enemy no matter where he was born. Dick Irvin was even worse. His dad, Dick Sr., had actually run the Leafs (he'd been among those behind the building of Maple Leaf Gardens), but had abandoned the team for Montreal, where he helped develop the Habs into a team that would prevent the Leafs from winning more Cups. As far as the boy was concerned, he was what some adults would have called a "Judas," who was a villain in the Bible. The James Boys called him "Dink" Irvin. He was a terrible person.

Once, the boy heard an announcer on television narrating a program about aliens and outer space and pyramids on the moon (*Chariot of the Gods*) who said, "You never know until you know." The idea of not knowing until you know something seemed rather obtuse— although the boy wouldn't have used that word; he would have said "dumb" or "lame" or "brainless"—but in the winter of 1975 the boy's idea of who the French were and what Quebec was like changed almost overnight. What happened was the Binghams' house on the bend of the boy's crescent went on sale, and, almost immediately a new family moved in, a family named the Brassards who came from Quebec. The Brassards had two kids: Melanie, a teenager, and John, who was twelve. Before meeting them, he expected the worst. Finding Habs fans in his school would have been a rare and terrible thing, but the thought of Habs fans and Habs kids on his street was almost too much to bear.

The first time the new kid came out of the house in his winter coat and boots to play street hockey, the boy was amazed to find that he looked nothing like either Xavier or George. He was square-shouldered with tousled blond hair and bright eyes, and he spoke English, which astonished the boy. When he asked him how come he knew English, he said, "Oh, lots of people in Quebec speak English." At first the boy thought he was a liar. But then Jimmy James said that if Keon spoke English, why wouldn't other people? The boy felt stupid for not putting this together, all the while relieved that he wouldn't have to speak French with his new street mate.

Because the boy was the biggest Leafs fan on the street—probably the biggest anywhere, he sometimes told himself—he had to ask the new kid about the Habs, and so, after hours playing in the cold sunshine of the winter's day, they sat together on a snowbank and the boy told him that he wasn't going to put up with listening to how great the Habs were because his street was a Leafs street and he better get used to it or else or else or else he didn't know what.

The new kid thought a moment.

"Well," he said, "what about the Expos?"

"What about them?" asked the boy.

"What do you think about the Expos?"

"Oh, I love the Expos."

"Great. Me too. We can be Expos fans together."

"Oh. Yeah, okay."

"Great."

"Okay. Great."

And that was that. They sat there for hours talking about something they both loved instead of something they hated. They talked about big tall caramel-skinned Ken Singleton and that crazy-fast Jerry White and little Tim Foli in the infield and Boots Day and Pepe Mangual and the new catcher, Gary Carter, who was gonna be good oh so good. John told the boy about Jarry Park and what it was like to see a real major league game in person, which the boy had always wanted to do but never had. He told him about seeing Tom Seaver pitch and Johnny Bench hit and Hank Aaron slug one out of the park for the Braves versus the Expos and how amazing the sounds were in real life instead of just on television. The new kid also talked about the Olympics—Montreal was scheduled to host the Games the next year—and how they were building this amazing stadium that would look like a spaceship and, if filled to the top, could hold seven trillion gold bricks or as much water as there was in all of James Bay. Suddenly Quebec sounded like a place with more than just dumb French things and people who wore gaylord clothes. Then the new kid's mother—an elegant woman named Murielle—came out in a long coat with fur around the collar and invited the two boys inside. She was tall with long eyelashes and a thin waist and long wavy hair, and inside she gave them something the boy had never heard of or seen called warm baguette, baked fresh out of the oven. The new kid's sister, Melanie, came to the kitchen table and she was beautiful: short hair with a perfect nose and lips like gummy worms. When she looked at you it was for a long time, straight on, which made the boy feel fantastic and unwell at the same time. The kid's father, who had a hilarious belly and a great booming voice, introduced himself and sat beside the boy. He stamped the flat of his hand on the table and said, "So tell me about these Maple Leafs of yours," then laughed a great laugh. Everyone else laughed, too, then started to talk loudly and at once. This almost never happened in the boy's home, especially not at dinnertime. The boy tore a piece of bread in half then stuffed it into his mouth. It was warm and dripping with butter. It tasted so good.

21

I knew that it wouldn't be hard to find Roscoe. Back in Toronto, a friend of mine mentioned him in passing, and I asked what he knew. The answer made me shiver. Roscoe was married and living in Whitby. He was a schoolteacher.

I sought counsel from others. I asked if they thought I should seek Roscoe out or confront him or invite him out for a coffee or a beer. Some said it would be interesting to see what he also remembered about that year, whether he felt burdened by the guilt of what he'd done. Then again, maybe he never thought about it, the memory sitting on the edge of his consciousness like a skiff barely visible on the curve of the horizon.

So much time had passed. The world and I had changed. Time raced where it once crawled; important things I knew were replaced by millions of other less important things I would never know; and Roscoe—the thug who had once corrupted my young world—was now in command of the same world, years later, with different kids. The Flyers hadn't won another Cup since 1975, while Dave Keon, the greatest Leaf ever, couldn't bring himself to return to the city that once embraced him as a hero. My dad was now old and my mom died of cancer when I was a teenager. We'd lived in a house in Etobicoke with my sister and our family dog. I'd gone to school at Dixon Grove, the school where it had all happened. It was tall and brown-bricked and loomed over the neighbourhood. I thought I should probably go there.

I drove for about twenty minutes through the city before passing into the suburbs—once new and fresh, but now less so—down Kipling Avenue, Etobicoke's main thoroughfare. As a boy—and more so as a teenager—I'd travelled down Kipling Avenue hundreds of times. The street that had delivered me in and out of my neighbourhood was lined with parks and homes and playgrounds and rinks, maybe one or two strip malls not yet weathered with the grime of suburban decay. It was along Kipling that I escaped the new suburbs for the dark frontier of the city, leaving a place that was once Valhalla for a kid whose only requirements were smooth asphalt, a stand of trees, and grass cut twice a month. At fourteen I found new friends, and it was among these friends that I shed the identity of a kid who'd been bullied for someone who moved freely and confidently through life, as if none of that had ever happened. I travelled with them down this suburban artery into the city after years of being terrified of downtown and all it represented. "Goin' to a show," I'd say on high school weekends, showing my parents the back of my head. They'd lower their cutlery and say, "Be careful," first my mom and dad, and then just my dad. That's all they said. It was enough.

I remembered evenings riding the Kipling 45 bus, sensing the lake as it got closer, tasting its cool moist air. I'd be wearing my dad's borrowed cool/uncool blazer, band pins running up the lapels, and sitting beside an open window watching yellow lamplights swoosh past like checkmarks against the ink of the sky. I'd started playing the guitar, doing shows. Every chord struck was an attempt to silence Roscoe, or the effect of him, or those like him. *Loserfaggotgeekhomogimpspaz.* Now I passed the forest where we used to get high before shows. I passed the bowling alley and I passed the neighbourhood's first strip mall, still standing. I could see the school now.

I parked the car on a street facing Dixon Grove. I looked out at the dead brown grass and remembered something that had happened to me before I decided to fight back. The day was like every other day after school: me lying on the lawn with Roscoe sitting on top, karate-chopping me in the neck or smushing my face into the dirt, calling me a queer or a loser and making me say shitty things about the Leafs. The Fuckin' Leafs. But it wasn't a memory of getting hurt or bullied that found me as I looked over the grass. It was the memory of the time Roscoe stopped hitting me, if only for a moment, after we'd talked about Reggie Leach.

A few years ago I'd met Leach, the "Riverton Rifle," in Whitehorse at another "Hockey Day in Canada," where I helped organize a concert at the local arts centre. My friend, musician John Samson of The Weakerthans, had started a petition to get the former Flyer into the Hockey Hall of Fame, and I'd asked John to come and play "Petition," his song about the player. Meanwhile the head of the local organizing committee, my friend Ranj, had invited Reggie, telling neither player nor musician about the other. John played his song, then the evening's host, CBC's Ron MacLean, invited Reggie onstage. Both men were thrilled to find the other there.

I stood in the wings when the Rifle came offstage. He held out his hand and I shook it. I thanked him for playing and he said, "That was a good song!" As he walked away I noticed the Stanley Cup rings on his hand, rings that had been won after terrorizing the Leafs and the rest of the league for two years. Still, that seemed okay. I'd loved hockey as a boy, and now, in my own way, I felt like I was part of it. Nothing that Roscoe had done to me stole from the poetry of the moment or the feeling of resolve I had after shaking hands with a member of a team I'd hated with all my soul. Instead it felt like a moment of triumph, but also vengeance. That was me standing next to Reggie Leach, not Roscoe. It was me he'd spoken to, not you, you fucking piece of shit. Fuck you. You were weak and I was strong and I had the mettle to rise into the beauty of life while you ended up a suburban drone too tired or weak-minded or weak-assed to terrify anyone—to challenge anyone—in your real life—your adult life—because you are fucking useless you piece of shit fuck you. You preyed on me and stole a year of my life and now look at yourself motherfucker. I am free because I won and you lost and I guess I should thank you but what I want to say is fuck you there I'll say it again and again and again fuck you you fucking piece of garbage.

I sat in front of the school pounding on the steering wheel. The car shook from the force of my hands. I screamed fuck you fuck you you fuckin' goddamned motherfucker. People passed on the street and, of course, no one came over. They hadn't before and they wouldn't start now. Fuck them. Fuck them all.

22

Through the February cold, Roscoe's drubbings abated. Even the thug found the conditions too grim for bullying. After school an army of kids slugged their way home wearing Bargain Harold's parkas and Hudson's Bay boots, their Adidas bags dragging behind them, plowing the sidewalk as the cold got bluer and the streets more grey, mountains of snow rising upon lawns, fields, and driveways. The average temperature was minus 4 degrees Fahrenheit (or 20 below Celsius, although Canadian kids didn't yet know that word) and sometimes, when it was too cold for snowballing or even street hockey, the boy spent his time clipping from his *Hockey Pictorials*. He'd paste the photos in his Hilroy scrapbook, making sure to use just enough glue so they'd stick but not so much that the paper thinned or rippled. The boy loved the way the glue splurted from the red nipple of the LePage bottle, and how it crusted like butterscotch at the tips of his fingers. Once he tried chewing the dried paste, but it tasted horrible, although something about the sweetly chemical smell kept his fingers pushed to his nose. Later that year, he saw an item on the news about kids who sniffed glue and how they ended up in some group home or the hospital, and so he stopped right away, even though the desire never left him.

Because of the dreadful cold, there were only a few good things about the winter of '75. One of those things was that his dad got tickets—greens—to see the Leafs play the California Golden Seals, who wore white skates and were the worst team in the league, with players named Len Frig and Dave Hrechkosy and Morris Mott and Jim Moxey. This meant that the Leafs would most likely win the game, making it extra good, although a bewildering 6–1 loss in Oakland had been the low point of a recent road trip. The boy had been to Maple Leaf Gardens before, but he would remember this game more than others because it happened on a weeknight. Staying up past bedtime was as good as Christmas or Halloween, and staying out late was even better. As a kid, being awake in the pulse of the late evening was like wandering the crust of a new planet, a wild journey informed by school fatigue and corrupted sleep patterns that made everything feel a little dreamy and strange. At night, colours were brighter, smells sharper, bodies bigger. Toronto was an Emerald City swimming in neon with bodies moving everywhere at once.

Storked on the landing, the boy's father snapped galoshes to his shoes while his mother brought the boy his church coat, demanding that he wear it. The boy would have argued in almost every other instance—the coat's sleeves scratched and its fabric gathered in all the wrong places—but he didn't because he agreed that going to see the Leafs was a special occasion, at least a trillion times better than church. The snow fell in fat clods from the sky as the boy and his father cleared the car, one of them scraping the windshield, the other pushing away snow with his wool mittens. The family owned a great silver-blue Buick with navy interior and power everything, and it roared to life as the boy's father turned the ignition, then slid the vehicle along the street to Kipling Avenue, where they headed south toward Eglinton through the cold dark night.

The windshield ice was slow to melt despite the car's roaring heater, so the boy's father was forced to peer through a small crescent in the glass, carefully working the steering wheel in gloved hands. Because the salt trucks hadn't yet found the suburbs, the car shimmied forward, its back end swinging out before the front end did the same. The roads were mostly empty and the Buick cruised alone in its lane, a good thing considering the wide swath they were cutting. The boy's father was never one to express concern no matter how precarious the situation— this was especially true of his boating captaincy, in which the family sometimes found themselves navigating rough waters—but he scrunched his face a little and tsked to himself as the snow fell in even heavier gobs. The car turned onto the South Kingsway—the fanciest street in the neighbourhood, with gingerbread awnings and long perfect driveways—and as they slid from stop sign to stop sign, the boy could hear his father sucking in air through his nose and sighing with concern. Winding out of the South Kingsway onto Bloor Street, he noticed the brilliant lights of the snow-roofed Old Mill subway station, a single long-coated figure standing outside its doors. Trying to be funny, he giggled and said, "Hey, we should take the subway to the game," even though he was loath to be anywhere other than in the warmth of the car. The boy's father looked at him and said, "Great idea!" He was going to tell him that he hadn't really meant it, but his father kept praising him. Eventually, the boy would feel proud of other things, too—getting good marks, scoring a goal at hockey, beating his cousins at pool—but he never felt as important as he did in that moment. A great idea. By a kid. It was his own.

Father and son parked the car and ran together to the station, their feet swooshing through the snow. While at the kiosk, the boy's father dug into his pocket looking for change, something he'd only ever seen his mother do at the supermarket or Smoke and Gift. As a rule, dads were about flat soundless bills that paid for necessities while moms were about the merry jangling of coins that produced gum and pop and hockey cards. Seeing his father count dimes and nickels in the enormous shell of his palm gave the boy pause. It was already a special night in so many ways.

Inside, the warm subway car was thick with bodies. It smelled of Export A tobacco and the sour odour of damp wool and musk, and even though it was crowded, hardly anyone spoke. Snow melted and water pooled at their feet as the boy and his father found two seats, and for a moment the quiet of the passengers nearly stilled the boy into slumber; only the rattling of the train kept him from falling asleep. Almost everyone in the car was male, most of them headed downtown for the hockey game. Back then, there was no other reason for anyone to be travelling into the city on a weeknight, and certainly no reason for a woman to be doing so. In the 70s, Toronto was an early-shuttered, temperate city, and if anything happened at all, it happened on Yonge Street, the throbbing main artery of a largely obstinate town. Without a game at the Gardens or a concert at Massey Hall, people headed to its taverns, strip bars, rock clubs, or porno theatres, maybe even a gay bathhouse like the St. Charles Tavern. The boy knew about the St. Charles because it's what the James Boys called Scott Carroll's house, implying that Carroll was gay (the boy also knew that you were never supposed to walk on the St. Charles side of Yonge unless you wanted people to know you were a homo). On Yonge Street people got stabbed and died doing drugs and jumped naked on fire through flophouse windows before landing bloodied on the streets below. The first time the boy ever went downtown was to visit the Simpsons department store at Queen and Yonge a few years before. The family had talked about the trip as if they were going to Damascus or Mumbai, preparing the boy and his sister for something they'd not yet experienced while growing up in the leafy bosom of their suburb. After being dropped off by his father, he stood next to his mother and sister outside the store and vomited on the sidewalk, sickened by the smell of diesel and the Molson's brewery on the Lakeshore, probably racked with anxiety, too. Afterward, the only times he ever went downtown were to visit his grandparents or go to Leafs games or the Canadian National Exhibition. Otherwise, he tried to stay away.

The subway moved past Jane, Dundas West, Ossington, Christie, and Bathurst, each station a little dirtier than the next. The boy studied the men standing by themselves who didn't look like hockey fans and wondered what they were doing and where they were headed. At a glance—he was careful not to stare—they seemed lost and sad. The boy thought that the best they could be was maybe not evil, not murderers or molesters or Hitler. It was a Wednesday night in February and they were going downtown. For sure, these men weren't getting into Heaven.

The train pulled into Carlton station and the crowd rushed out, marching together up the steps of the subway to the street above, which bloomed with action. If everyone else in the city had already settled into their solemn evenings at home, the corner of Yonge and Carlton roared with life: pennant vendors, program sellers, and a swarm of scalpers whose voices snapped at the air. People moved across traffic and around a few slowly crawling cars to the front of the rink, hips and elbows and the stomachs of strangers pinching the boy and pulling him forward. Gripping his father's hand tighter with each step, he could see the Gardens' marquee come into view—GAME TONIGHT LEAFS V CALIFORNIA—its fitted blue letters predating the pixel board that would replace it years later. Getting through the glass doors at the front of the rink was an even greater task: hundreds of winter-jacketed men moving into the arena at once. The smell of popcorn and ammonia filled his senses, and suddenly everything was bright and people all around him were talking. The boy thought he could hear the sound of pucks hitting the boards, but wasn't sure.

The boy's father bought two Cokes with plastic lids and straws, a sleeve of Fruitella, and a box of popcorn, the kind with the drawing of an elephant pedalling a beach ball (another great thing about staying out late: snacks past the boy's bedtime). Settling into his tiny seat—too small for most adults, but perfect for the boy—he saw that the ice was the colour of egg whites, the yellow of the TV lamps tinting the surface just so. The arena seats were gold, red, green, and grey—rich, if dour, colonial shades—while the end blues hung over the far end of the rink above the goals, perfect for catching pucks deflected after slapshots taken from the point, mostly by Ian Turnbull, who hadn't yet learned to control his shot. A large pale scoreboard with gold numbers hung above centre ice and the organist played "Hello Dolly." There was some mumbling in the crowd and then the sound of a metal door arm being clanked open in a deep corner of the rink. Through the door, three referees stepped out and began skating around the ice. The organist stopped playing "Hello Dolly" and started "Three Blind Mice." The crowd's mumbling turned to booing and his father gently elbowed the boy. The boy laughed through cheeks stuffed with popcorn.

Pretty soon, the Golden Seals—who actually looked more green than gold—appeared near the visitors' bench. There was a bit more booing, but less than for the refs, which seemed strange to the boy. After a few moments the Leafs came out. They cruised blue-shouldered about the ice, hair swept back, sticks clacking as they skated. The boy's heart leapt into his mouth. Going faster with each lap around their zone—moving first behind the net, then out across the red line—the players seemed excited to be travelling at such speeds: darting between each other, ducking and swooping, shwacking at pucks dumped out of a bucket like cat paws after a spill of mice.

The Leafs had found themselves short-staffed after a series of unfortunate episodes during their road trip, where they'd gone 0–4 after a rare victory over Montreal at the Forum. In Vancouver, Jim McKenny suffered what writer Frank Orr said was "a freak accident" that came "after the end of a skate lace which McKenny uses to hold his suspenders and shoulder pads together whipped up and hit his eye, causing an abrasion to the cornea." The boy had winced when he read this, although later in life he'd weigh such a report with suspicion, having learned to read sportswriters' code, knowing that injuries weren't always what they seemed. The boy would become a man who would hear stories about the rookie forward who'd missed five games with a hamstring pull, but had actually been beaten up by an angry, vengeful drug dealer in an alley after a coke buy gone bad; or the injured defenceman out for the season who'd in fact crossed a member of a local biker gang after sleeping with his girlfriend; or the goalie who'd reportedly injured his back during practice but had actually tweaked his disc after a wild tryst with two female servers in a local pub; or the time three Adams Division players were benched purportedly for bad play when what they'd really done was spend the evening in jail after trying to stop a pimp from assailing one of his charges on a late-night Winnipeg run. Still, to an eleven-year-old, McKenny's story seemed plausible. A skate lace. Those things were pretty sharp.

Other players were missing, too. George Ferguson's hand was in a cast, the result, wrote Orr, of an Oakland hotel-room altercation between Ferguson and his roommate, Tiger Williams. In his book *Tiger,* the player described how, wanting to help enforce the team's 11 p.m. curfew because of the way they'd been playing, he tried to stop Ferguson from going out. "He was swearing and blustering, and I just pushed him down on the bed and said that if he didn't stop, I would hit him really hard. There was lots of noise and players came in the room to see what was happening. [Later] Ferguson went off to Dunc Wilson's room, and then somebody put a call into [coach] Red Kelly. Before Kelly appeared, Ferguson came out of Wilson's room holding his hand. It was broken." Orr wrote how Ferguson "had [thrown] the only punch before Williams pushed him onto a bed and the scrap was broken up"; and as Williams told the *Star*, "I wasn't expecting it and Fergie hit me with a good punch. The team is losing and sometimes nerves get frayed." (Although Williams said in his book that Ferguson had gone into Wilson's room and "flailed around, smashing his hand against the wall.") The boy would become a man who would be astonished that this sort of thing was ever reported in the papers. There was one thing, however, that wasn't reported. Arriving home, Keon called a meeting between Kelly and his players. Things were getting out of hand and they had to be stopped.

The team was also missing Lanny McDonald (pulled muscle), Brian Glennie (finger tendon), Bob Neely (bruised ankle), Eddie Shack (assigned to minors), and goalie Dunc Wilson (suspended for breaking curfew on the road trip)—but there were still lots of curious cases in the lineup. The boy wanted to see Claire Alexander because of his name—Did he skate like a girl? Did he look like one?—and because the thirty-three-year-old player had made the Maple Leafs after years playing senior hockey with the Orillia Terriers. He also wore a small bucket helmet—a Jofa—and even better, he'd been a cottage-country milkman before signing with the Leafs. Studying him from the greens, it was true that Alexander looked a bit different from the other players; he was certainly older, and he wore his hair clipped short while so many of the others had long sideburns or afros that bobbed when they skated.

The boy picked off every player as they warmed up, beginning and ending, naturally, with Keon. The captain didn't skate quite as hard or fast as the other players, yet he seemed just as strong on his feet, maybe even stronger. He held his stick at his waist while moving around the ice, back bent and head down, only occasionally looking up. His hair seemed blacker than black and his sweater bluer than blue when he stopped near centre ice and looked down at the Seals at the end of the rink. Other players were taller; many were wider. Yet the captain was the physical focus of everyone in the arena.

Keon commanded the ice despite being only five-foot-nine, 163 pounds. He was small, yet feared, and if not feared, at least respected. The boy wondered what it would have felt like to skate above one's height, to possess great power even though you weren't powerfully built. At eleven, the boy's body was changing every day, moulting out of his child's frame into a young man's, which made it impossible for him to feel confident in his skin. His baby fat was disappearing—replaced by stiff, new muscle—and bone that was once soft and pliable had hardened and forced itself into joints that didn't quite fit. There was very little harmony to the pace of his growth. Some body parts grew while others did not, creating a FrankenBoy of floppingly large feet and clamshell ears and a neck that suddenly popped out of his shoulders. His nose swelled where the rest of his face did not and his lips bloomed as his chin retreated into his skull. The same was true of his friends. Jimmy James suddenly developed strong biceps that mismatched his chicken chest and Little Johnny's thighs exploded while his waist remained girlishly small. Together they jumbled about like a bag of sticks and rocks at a time when some kids had grown faster and fitted together better. Roscoe, for instance, had willed his body to maturity, but when the boy tried this, he grew larger in all the wrong places, never tall and menacing, only bulbous and wonky, a plaything at the mercy of nature's folly.

During the anthems—"Star Spangled Banner" first, and then "O Canada," both played by Ralph Fraser on the organ—the crowd stood quietly, barely a sound coming from the seats. People were respectful of the precious beauty of the Gardens, comporting themselves as if visiting an aunt in her dotage whose only purpose in life was to maintain the fine austerity of her sitting room. As the players had gathered at centre ice there'd been a little cheering—none of it prompted by music or exploding scoreboards or a mascot parading among the stands, shopworn triggers of the modern game—but otherwise the crowd was still, its near-silence an occasional source of embarrassment for critics, who compared Toronto fans with those in Montreal. But it was this sense of quiet that produced the boy's most sustaining memory of watching Dave Keon play, a memory that his father would talk about years later, for he'd remembered it, too.

It began like any other play: a line change during the relative slumber of the second period. Defenceman

Turnbull threw the puck up the right boards from the Leafs' end, and it rattled against the plywood before skipping over a Seals defenceman's stick and leaving the zone. The Californians retreated to fetch the puck, and if the Leafs forwards considered moving on them they soon thought better of it, streaming toward the bench for a line change. At this the captain hurdled the boards, landing skates flat to the ice. A Seals player threw the puck up the ice to a teammate who'd remained during the Leafs' change, but such were the Seals' fortunes—and their level of ability—that the puck easily missed the open player. It ended up on Börje Salming's stick a few feet inside the Leafs' blue line.

Salming looked up the ice—a gesture like a thousand others in the dozen games happening that night, but because it came from Salming it was different, and so was the play that followed. The Swedish defenceman had been with the team for his rookie year, but fans still weren't used to him. Salming stared out through sad, cautious eyes. He had smooth alabaster skin, a long, luminous face with Roman-column cheekbones, and a jaw like a bear trap. He skated wide-legged as if walking through a bog with his pants hitched above the ankle, and had a wingspan that contained almost any defender who chanced to move into his corner. Standing along the blue line during a power play, he'd cock his stick above his waist to shoot before the puck was delivered (usually by his partner, Ian Turnbull), the first person in the NHL to employ such broad exaggeration. Teammates also talked about

Salming's shoulder strength and core power, a European athleticism that resulted from a fitness routine based on running and stretching and a diet of grains and proteins. This routine would become the norm thirty or forty years later, but in 1975 it produced a lean, elastic body type in stark contrast to the medicine ball, steak- and pasta-fed skaters who populated the league. The boy would grow to be a man who would listen to former Leafs goalie Doug Favell tell him: "During our first game in Philadelphia I knew they'd be going after Börje, so I told him, 'They're gonna try to intimidate you; you're gonna have to stand up to them.' I told him that [Dave] Schultz could only throw with his right hand and to get ahold of his shoulder. Once Schultz made his move—the crowd was yelling 'Kill the Swede! Kill the Swede!'—Börje did what I'd said, and he was so strong and his arms so long that he just held the player. Schultz never even threw a punch."

If Salming had learned his game among fit, like-minded cousins in the Swedish pro league, here he was surrounded by hardscrabble farm boys and milkmen who'd made the NHL by virtue of their grit and resilience. Sweet-skating forwards who lived in the open ice might have been the norm in European hockey, but they were the exception in an NHL dominated by tough cornermen and players who earned their paycheques scoring from the slot, to say nothing of rushless defencemen who let the responsibility fall to two rearguards—Brad Park and Bobby Orr—to score while the rest stayed home. In Linköping or Timrå or Växjö or Gothenburg or Karlstad, a typical game would have inevitably found a breaking forward swirling up ice waiting for Salming's pass, but here it wasn't necessarily a given. Canadian players were happier chasing a puck bounding into the depths of the corner than swinging east-west along the red line. Hockey was traditional and informed with Canadian conservatism. Chances weren't taken and pucks were smothered or stilled rather than flung wildly to a breaking forward.

The boy saw Salming look up the ice. The player's eyes widened as he heard a sound—"Hawwwww!!!"—coming from in front of the Leafs bench. It was Keon speeding down the ice, yelling for the pass. Later in his life, the boy would become a man who would ask himself whether he'd ever heard a more Canadian sound in a more Canadian place: "Hawwwww!!" An Irish accent passed over a northern tongue. "Hawwwww!!" One boy in a sweater shouting to another boy in a sweater across the howling wind. "Hawwwww!" Neil Young in his fringe jacket calling the end of a long solo. "Hawwwww!!" What Relic said after finding a bounty of salvage that Nick was too Greek to find.

"Hawwwww!!"

Salming brought the puck to his skate heel and fired it up the ice. Keon caught it CLAPP! on the flat of his blade. The boy and his father lurched forward in their seats. The captain moved in on goal and shot at the Seals goalie, Gary Simmons, who made the save with his glove then fell to his knees before placing his glove between his pads and lowering his head to stop play. Keon skated away, stick crossed at his knees. The boy looked at his father and his father looked at the boy, aware of what they'd just seen and heard. Later on, walking tired-legged out of the Gardens through falling snow into the subway station, the boy asked himself why, instead of goals or assists or who'd won the game (Leafs 4, Seals 2), he would remember this play more than any other, a play that had happened between other plays. Maybe that was part of being a writer, too.

23

Sitting at my desk in my perfectly nice kitchen in my perfectly nice house with my perfectly nice family sleeping upstairs, I wrote:

"It took some time, but I calmed down. I felt the blood leave my face and my fists unclench. I left Dixon Grove for the highway pointing east, knowing I'd never go back there, not ever. I drove along the 401 past Don Valley, Scarborough, and Pickering then exited the ramp in the direction of Whitby, fuckin' Whitby. A few days earlier I'd found some information online about Roscoe: the name of his school, how long he'd been there (eight years), and whether he'd ever been named District Teacher of the Year (he had, once, in 2005). Not only that, but I found out that he taught English: English literature. I wondered if his class had ever studied, say, *Lord of the Flies,* and whether he'd paused at the sections where Jack terrorizes

Piggy. I wondered if he ever looked out at the kids seated in straight narrow rows pointing at him and wondered which kid was him and which was me and whether he should help that kid, or at least make sure the class knew exactly what the book was about, although maybe the kids could already sense in the gummy sinew of their thoughts that whenever the teacher talked about Jack he was talking about himself, seeing how his throat closed a little and his shoulders tightened trying to get through the character study as quickly as possible. Or maybe none of this was true. Maybe the teacher worked his way through the book resolutely, dispassionately, expressing nothing, lazy fucking coward.

"Off the highway, I found myself driving through a bland suburban neighbourhood. It looked like Etobicoke only with a few more drive-thrus and newer strip malls with aestheticians and dog groomers and health food stores; identikit homes, too, but with wide lots and two cars—one an SUV, always an SUV—sitting speckless and black in long smooth driveways. The day was grey but there was a kind of muted shine to the neighbourhood, as if everyone had moved in at the same time and bought their stuff at the same store that sold stuff marked up and too expensive. Very few people were around. It was quiet, midday. Lunchtime. I turned the corner as the school— Willowcrest—came into view.

"I parked opposite the school's main doors, turning the engine off. I didn't know what Roscoe looked like, or whether I'd recognize him. It had been more than forty years. In my imagination, his ass had swollen and his face had been devoured by his bloated cheeks and a sagging forehead: no eyes, nose, or teeth, either, just disgusting folds on a once-able body that had been Coked and doughnuted to near-death after a sad life of cable TV and PokerStars. Watching him waddle back to school carrying an embarrassment of fast-food bags would be to observe that fate and time had done my work for me and that extracting any sort of physical tax from him would prove empty and unfulfilling.

"I looked out the window and saw one teacher, then another. None of them looked like Roscoe. I wanted to observe him—maybe confront him—for a lot of reasons, but mostly because I wanted an ending to the story that I would tell my hero. Keon would ask me, 'So whatever happened to Roscoe, anyway?' while sitting on the patio looking at the ocean eating chicken poppers and drinking beer. I'd tell him that I'd found Roscoe at a school where he worked: a schoolteacher; yes, I know. I'd tell him that because I'd found Roscoe I could move on, and because I'd moved on, he could, too, returning to Toronto to lead the Maple Leafs to their first Stanley Cup in fortysomething years. Yonge Street. Confetti. Doves. Small children holding blue and white flags. Wendel Clark would be there. So would Börje Salming and Jim McKenny and Vesa Toskala and Frank Bialowas and Harold Druken and Val James and Toots Holway and Sailor Herbert and Pat Boutette and Steve Kraftcheck and Craig Muni and Norm Aubin and Turk Broda and Mariusz Czerkawski and Rocky

Dundas and Cory Cross and Ernie Godden and Pat Hickey and Ron Hurst and Shep Mayer and René Robert and Garry Valk and Clarke Wilm and Nathan Dempsey and Aki Berg and Gerald Diduck and Stew Gavin and Dick Gamble and Bruce Gamble and Rick Lanz and Don Luce and Bingo Kampman and Wes Jarvis and Dave Manson and Yanic Perreault and Bob Parent and Ben Ondrus and Ric Nattress and Glenn Anderson and Darryl Maggs and Lonny Bohonos and Dan Maloney and Adam Mair and Val James and Frank Nighbor and Bryan McCabe and Bob Manno and Denis Dupéré and Benoît Hogue and Scott Garland and Kirk Muller and Don Metz and Nick Metz and Rudy Migay and Robert Reichel and Basil McRae and Eric Lacroix and Ric Jackman and Peter Ing and Benny Grant and Errol Thompson and Brad Smith and Tim Ecclestone and Hal Gill, and, of course, Syl Apps and Terry Sawchuk and King Clancy, all of whom would rise from the Great Beyond. Dave Keon would be at the front of the march. This would almost certainly happen.

"A few more teachers appeared, and many more kids. And then, coming from around the side of the building, two teachers, a woman and a man, possibly husband and wife. My heart climbed into my throat. It beat hard as it settled there. Before coming to the school—to his school—I'd thought seeing him would trigger an angry, hot, palpitating sweat and a shivering of the bones, all those feelings of terror and regret returning to me at once.

"But in that moment staring out from the car, I surprised myself by how calm and settled I felt. Time had crawled ahead and life had changed and we were now both adults living in adult worlds. However tethered to the experiences of childhood, I saw in that moment that neither of us had been doomed to remain the people we'd been all those years ago. Having spent the previous six to eight months living inside the mind and soul of whoever I'd been at eleven, I was prepared for this moment. I had devoured my pain moving forward—more distant each day from the person I'd been the day before—and sitting in the car, I looked out at the face of the school feeling gratified and proud that I'd done what I'd done: reliving an episode in my life I would have preferred not to remember. I was done with that. I was done with him. Fuck it. It was over.

"I wasn't even sure it was him. It had been so long and we'd both changed so much. But I thought it was. Standing there, the two of them looked like married teachers, and while they'd always wanted children, it had never worked out. The woman had a face like a small pretty bird in a short dark cloak. The man was considerably larger and also wore a cloak, dark brown. A toque was pushed on his head. His angry, terrifying eyes had softened and found light, and if Roscoe had moved through middle school like a sullen and angry beast, he was now pleasantly adult, calmly mannered, and average in appearance.

"The man and his wife stopped and spoke to a few kids—all girls—directing them inside. He said something and the girls laughed and then the woman laughed, too. Then another man—he was older, with white hair—came out and put his hand on the man's shoulder. He spoke and the man nodded: 'I just wanted to tell you, Roscoe, that you've been nominated once again for District Teacher of the Year. I think this year could be your year. I mean, after all you've done for the kids, and for the school.' The older man went inside. The couple lingered by the doors for a second and the woman grabbed the man's hand hanging at his side. She squeezed it.

"I watched them go into the school, knowing that, even if he was who I thought he was—and even if he wasn't—it no longer mattered. I'd lived with him through the writing of this book, and because I'd kept going without giving in to the recurring pain of those times, I knew I didn't have to confront him—I'd already done that while craning over my screen and notepad, trying to figure out what had happened forty years ago. I was a man and he was a man. And, in the end, it was left to me to tell our story. This was my life. This was my work. I turned on the car. I drove home."

24

To the boy, mornings were the worst, but Sunday mornings were even worse than that. Just a few years earlier he would have been rolling around on the carpet at 5:30 a.m., playing army with his toys or shaking his mom's shoulder in bed begging for cereal or buttered toast, but since he was growing fast the weekend's sleep found him pinned exhausted to his dreams. On Saturday mornings he slept until road hockey, but Sundays were church mornings, and even though the boy knew that going to church and being a good person and not stealing or lying or hurting other people was how you got into Heaven, it didn't make getting up any easier. Going to church was made a little less terrible if the Leafs had won the night before—he could busy his mind going over exciting plays in his head as a way of blotting out the monotonous voice of the old bald priest—but because he had to wear stupid tight ugly brown and grey clothes and sit on a hard bench called a "pew" listening to the priest say things the boy didn't understand, it was torturous. Nobody else in his family seemed happy being there either, but if the boy wanted to stay out of Hell—if any of them wanted to stay out of Hell—it was something he had to do. This was what the Catholic Church believed and because the Catholic Church ran St. Michael's College where Dave Keon had played hockey, he must have believed it, too.

In Brian McFarlane's book about the Leafs, the boy had read about the captain's early days at St. Mike's; how he lived in the St. Clair Avenue residence and played at the old rink on Bathurst Street, which the boy and his family sometimes drove past on their way to his grandparents' house in the city. Later in life, the boy would become a man who would talk to former Leaf and Olympian Terry Clancy, who'd played at St. Mike's at the same time as Keon. Clancy remembered "looking out the window of my residence into the principal's office across the way and watching Dave Keon get married to his first wife, Lola." At St. Mike's, Keon played for Father Bauer, who taught a game based on principles that would become common in the NHL only years later: defensive responsibilities, zone coverage, and an athletic comportment based on respect, discipline, and the ability to turn the other cheek whenever the game became violent, trading in an eye-for-an-eye mentality for a quiet toughness, a quality that Keon possessed throughout his career. In a way, the boy thought the captain played a very Christian game, understanding that, at the end of his days, he'd be judged by how he carried himself on the ice. The same was true of a lot of players who'd gone to St. Mike's—Frank Mahovlich, Tim Horton, and Red Kelly, to name three—and although the boy hated admitting it, players who came from Quebec were the same way because, in Quebec, as in Italy, the only religion was Catholic. This partly explained why the Flyers were so evil. A lot of their fighters came from the prairies, where there was no Catholic Church or moral code and you could do anything you wanted.

Sometimes the boy worried about what God was thinking whenever he privately asked himself why he was doing what he was doing on Sunday mornings. Whenever bad thoughts entered his head, he squinched his eyes and folded his brow and tightened his fists, burying them in some dark chamber of his mind. Because God could see and hear everything, he wondered whether any of these thoughts ever slipped past Heaven—Did they collect them? Did they store them away and look at them later?—especially thoughts about how church smelled like bad breath and how the adults always looked tired and defeated until they were told to shake hands, and even then they were mostly smiling because church was about to end. Sometimes the boy found Little Johnny or Guido sitting in the pews, but their parents separated them because they were trouble together. Since the James Boys' mom wasn't the get-up-early type, the brothers almost never had to go to church. In the long run, this was both a good and a bad thing. It was good because they got to sleep in, but it was also bad because it meant that when St. Peter opened his book, their attendance record would probably be noted. Things would be a little more dicey for them in Heaven.

The boy wanted to do right by God—he never talked back and he listened to his teachers and parents and he never stole or did anything like that—but because these kinds of thoughts came to him more regularly with age—partly because of what Roscoe was doing to him and partly because he was seeing a little deeper into the world—he worried about the consequences. It was the first complication in a life full of them, but it also meant that he was growing up.

The following Saturday yielded the first heavy snowfall of the year. Everything was bright and soft and packed down on the roads, promising a fast surface for street hockey, which the boy played every opportunity he got. He got dressed, scooped a bowl of Cheerios into his mouth, climbed into his green shell of a winter coat, tied his boots to his feet, collected his small brown pads, gloves, mask, and goalie stick, and plungered his toque on his head before running into the street.

The James Boys were there first: shovelling a clearing and setting up nets at opposite ends of the rink. Jimmy and Walter's Saturday mornings were usually the same routine: Pop Tarts for breakfast and a cup of instant coffee for their mom, which they made then put quietly on her bedside table, the coffee growing cold before she'd wake up hours later. The James Boys had learned to do things on their own, and if Walter felt hard done by, Jimmy had grown into his responsibilities, both emotionally and physically. He had the biggest biceps of any of the boys and a neck almost adult in its breadth. Because he was the oldest male at home, he'd been forced to trade book smarts for a kind of learned savvy but was more quietly confident than anyone else in the pack, knowing that exposed weakness would leave him weak in the heart and sad for a mom who couldn't get out of bed. The boy wouldn't have called Jimmy "tough" because he didn't go around fighting other kids. He was tough in a different way, in a quiet way, in a way the boy thought was more honourable than Roscoe's kind of tough, which wasn't tough at all.

Clomping down the street in his boots, the boy saw Little Johnny, then Guido, then Scott Carroll, then Frank Martello moving from the other end of the street toward the game. After everyone had arrived the James Boys told them that they'd invited a bunch of kids from another street to play against them.

"Like an actual game?" asked Little Johnny.

"Yeah, I guess so," said Walter.

"What are the rules gonna be?" asked Scott.

"Who cares?" said Walter. "You ever heard of one street challenging another street to a game of road hockey?"

"Never happens," said Johnny.

"Besides, we'll kick their ass," said Walter.

"Darned right we will," said Jimmy. "'Dave's in net, okay?"

The boy had already dropped to the road to put on his equipment. Playing goal in street hockey suited him because of how good it felt using his entire body to make saves, even though he'd taken more than a few shots to the balls. Still, he liked the time spent in his own head—in this way, it wasn't so different from writing—falling into a mental and physical thrum whenever the play scrambled around him, the ball skipping along the ground and through the air. While it proved challenging to move about on the ice—his ankles were never quite strong enough to keep up with other players—in road hockey his feet were freed from their skates, sliding across the surface the way they did on the carpet at home while watching the Leafs. He thought of this as he tightened the straps on his pads to his trousered legs, fitted his gloves on his hands—one a first baseman's mitt with Joe Torre's fine, dark signature on the thumb, the other a Tony Esposito waffle board— and righted his slasher-film mask on his face, instantly warming his cold cheeks as he rose a few pounds heavier to his feet, telling the other players, "Okay, shots," waving at them with his enormous, flopping glove.

"Shots."

His teammates lined up and moved in on him, spanking the faded green tennis ball at the net. The boy's arms and legs felt loose, the warmth of his blood oiling his joints as shots came one after another: *poam! shwapp! thumbk!!* Soon, voices came from around the bend in the crescent. The boys turned to see the other team, sticks tipped musket-style across their shoulders, walking down the street. There was only one kid among them who wasn't smiling the giddy smile of Saturday morning in the winter playing a game he loved. The boy couldn't believe it.

Roscoe.

The bully was easily the tallest player on his team. When he'd first set eyes on the boy, he'd pointed down the street and laughed a great terrible laugh, mocking and harsh. Jimmy said they should probably go up to their opponents and say hello, but the boy had another idea: "I need more shots." So Jimmy took it upon himself to greet the other team, where Roscoe, standing at the front of the group, asked if the goalie was who he thought he was. The older James Boy said yes and Roscoe laughed again, spittle spraying from his mouth. "This is gonna be fuckin' easy, shooting on that gimp!" he said. Jimmy, expressing himself in a dadless way the boy never could have mustered, said, "You can shut up about that now." Roscoe paused for a moment, looking as if he was about to punch Jimmy. "We'll see who does the shutting up," he said, turning away.

Jimmy called the team to gather around the boy's goal. Frank Martello—the Italian kid whose parents spoke with an accent—would play defence and so would Scott Carroll. The James Boys would play up front with Little Johnny, and Guido would be the first sub. The other team had another kid—tall and long-legged with a great swoosh of blond hair—who looked athletic, but other than him and Roscoe, the teams were physical equals. Before the game started, the blond kid told Jimmy James, "We're called the Silvercreek Atoms, just so you know." Jimmy said, "Yup, I know," even though he didn't, "and so just *you* know, we're the Warbeck Warriors." The blond kid said, "Hey, that's a decent name," which, in 1975, meant the name was good.

The boy knew that playing goal in an important game wouldn't be easy, but Roscoe's presence made things twice as hard, more so considering that street hockey was supposed to be a place of freedom and liberty, his *sanctuary*, which was a word he'd learned from the movie *The Hunchback of Notre Dame*, played on Buffalo TV twice a year or so. This was to say nothing of how the game might affect what happened every weekday at 3:30 p.m., even though he was probably doomed with or without the game. If he beat Roscoe's team, the thug would likely seek retribution on the cold turf outside the school, but if he threw the game, he'd probably get hit for being shit at hockey. Once the match started—Jimmy had used the point of his toothpick blade to carve a centre-ice circle in the middle of the road—it became clear that the bully was a formidable presence, lumbering like a huge clunking trunk up and down the street, holding out an arm and swatting players away like King Kong batting at buzzing jetfighters.

The boy played poorly for the first half hour. He gave up three early goals, two of them to Roscoe, who cackled and swore as he hop-stepped, hands in the air, the green ball lying like a bruised apple in the folds of the mesh. Jimmy said to the boy, tapping his pads, "Let's not let Foghorn Leghorn beat us, all right?" It was a funny thing to call Roscoe. The boy wanted to laugh out loud, but could not.

Moments later the Atoms scored again after Scott Carroll lost the ball in his feet. Carroll was as much of a liability in sports as he was in life. If he wasn't breaking a neighbour's window with a baseball he was accidentally crushing his foot, which he did while trying to move a stack of cinder blocks in his parents' garage looking for his dad's *Playboys* (they weren't even there, it turned out). Scott was once rushed to the hospital after drinking turpentine, and another time he fell off his bike into an open sewer. The kid moved around as if oblivious to where he was or what he was doing, his eyes glazing over, mouth hanging open. Back then, nobody recognized these as the signs of an imaginative mind; everyone thought Scott was just duh and kind of slow. Straight A's in science and math meant little to those for whom falling into a sewer was the essence of failure.

Until the fourth goal, the boy had never had a problem with Scott Carroll, but because of the game's circumstances—and because playing against Roscoe made him feel sick—he lost his temper in the crease, throwing his gloves and sticks down and yelling at the defenceman for being a useless dork and saying everybody laughs at you you useless spaz. The boy's face was hot and his chest grew tight and his throat felt sore after forcing out the words. Scott said, "I'm sorry," having heard these kinds of things before. The older James Boy collected the equipment and walked over to Carroll, telling him that it was okay. Jimmy asked the boy, "What's with Foghorn Leghorn? He says he knows you or something." The boy wanted to tell him everything, but he couldn't, at least not then. "Let's just play," he said, slipping on his gloves, which had grown moist with sweat despite the cold. "Let's get one back."

The Warriors pressed into the Atoms' end. Their goalie was small and wore an oversized winter coat, which the boy thought was clever: wearing his brother's clothes to cover more of the net. The boy hadn't thought of doing this himself, and because he hadn't, he was forced to fight the notion that he was somehow inferior to his opposite. It didn't help, either, when the small goalie punted away Jimmy James's shot from just in front of the snowbank onto Mr. Fenwick's lawn. "Time!" yelled one of the Atoms as he ran in his boots to get it. Collecting the ball near the curb, he flung it to another player, who scooped it toward the net. The boy's glove swooshed through the air as he caught the ball on a rise before holding it tight to his heaving chest. It was something: a good save. It was a start.

More saves followed, then a few more, and after the James Boys scored twice each, the Warriors found themselves having drawn even in the game. Frank Martello scored after that, and then Guido curved one in, and soon the boy's team was ahead by two goals. At this point Roscoe did what he'd always done whenever the boy had played against him on the ice: carrying the puck by himself as if no one else was playing. This allowed the Warriors to besiege the lumbering, sour-face giant with a kind of blanket defence, which isn't to suggest that Roscoe didn't get his shots, or his goals. In fact, because he was so much more physically mature than everyone else, he forced his way through the defence, scoring twice on shots that not even Bernie Parent could have stopped. Still, the boy considered it a small victory when, after Roscoe screamed the ball into the far corner of the net, the thug turned away, forgetting to cackle or laugh or call the boy a sieve or a gimp or a spaz or whatever other words he used to prove how great and mean and tough he was.

Time passed and the boys kept playing. They ignored lunch as the day leaned into mid-afternoon. The sun grew smaller, dimming the winter light. The game went from having a two-goal difference to being tied and then back again, until suddenly Roscoe scored one goal, then another, then another, putting the Atoms ahead 17–14 at a time when the creeping late-day cold made it seem as if the end of the game was closer than the beginning. Someone from the Atoms said, "Stop at four?" Everyone agreed, leaving about forty minutes left to play. There was a break as the teams plunked down in snowbanks, filling their mouths with snow in the absence of food and drink.

"I'm gonna take a run at the big one," said Walter. "I'm gonna get at his knees."

"You've been trying that all day," said his brother. "Still won't work. He's too tall."

"Well," he said, "I'll stab him in the balls."

"You've been doing that, too."

"Man, I hate that guy," said Frank Martello.

"Nobody hates him more than Dave," said Jimmy. "Am I right?"

The boy said nothing.

"You know him or something?" asked Walter. "He go to your school?"

"No," the boy mumbled.

"But he knows your name," said Jimmy.

The boy stared at the ground, his gloves at his sides.

"Actually, I know him," said Scott Carroll. The words made the boy freeze.

"Yeah," he continued, "I know him because when his mom was sick my mom helped his mom and once I went over to his house to play and you know, like, keep him company. We played some board games and watched television. He was actually a kind of quiet guy. Not nice, but not not nice if you get me."

The boy had never thought of Roscoe having a mom, let alone one that was sick, let alone spending time with Scott Carroll in his basement playing board games.

Walter asked Scott: "Why's he such a dick then? I mean, besides being pissed off having to hang out with you."

"I dunno," said Scott. "His mom ended up dying. Cancer. Maybe he's just sad. People act funny after bad things happen to them."

"That makes him a wuss," blurted Walter, interrupting a train of thought shared by the others: that bad things had also happened to the James Boys.

"He's not a wuss," said Jimmy. "He's just another player. And we're not going to let him beat us." With that, Jimmy stood up. The boy could tell what his dadless friend was thinking: that even though there were times when his mother seemed as if she wasn't there—falling silent, especially after one of his dad's annual visits, where he'd bring the boys gifts they'd already outgrown—Jimmy hadn't let it poison him. Jimmy knew there was something weak and sad in Roscoe because there was something weak and sad in him, too, and while he hadn't let it change him, it had turned Roscoe into a bully. The boy had only ever seen Roscoe as strong and terrible, but after seeing him through his friends' eyes, he became less than that. Just a kid. A kid whose mother had died of cancer, which is what would happen to the boy's mother, although nobody would know that, not yet. Standing up, the boy thought a moment. *Everybody is sad together.* He didn't know why he thought of this. He just did.

The game started again. Kids on both teams ran exhausted and breathless up and down the road. They chopped at the ball from every angle, but because they were tired and sore-legged, there were very few close or clean shots, making the goalies' job a little easier. Because the boy was cold, he moved about whenever the play was up the road, whirling his arms around like a nervous scarecrow, kicking his legs out like a tiny Rockette. After twenty minutes neither team had scored, and after twenty more it remained tied. Then, as the game wound down, Roscoe gathered the ball in his end and charged. He ran head down, legs choogling along the road. The boy's teammates threw themselves at the player, but they were tumbleweeds in his path. Nearing the goal, Roscoe wound up, his stick raised behind him to meet the plane of his shoulders. Closing the gap, Jimmy James lunged from behind, tripping the bully before his stick could swat at the ball. Roscoe went down hard. The two boys came together standing up, and it looked like there'd be a fight. The boy imagined what would happen: his dadless friend beating the living snot out of the bully, leaving him crumpled and broken and bleeding on the road as the kids stood above him whacking and clubbing him with their sticks.

The two boys moved toward each other, but the blond kid on the other team yelled, "Penalty shot!" Roscoe and Jimmy James froze. His teammates turned to the boy, who stood in the crease trying not to puke.

He nodded.

Penalty shot.

The boy had prayed before, although he'd mostly prayed because he'd been told to. He'd prayed the way any little kid does: kneeling at the bed in pyjamas asking God to look over his mom and dad and sister and the family dog, maybe even the Leafs, especially the Leafs. He'd said his prayers in a singsong bedtime voice with his parents standing on the other side of his bedroom door listening with joy to the uncomplicated melodies of their son. As a child, the boy spoke to God in a whisper, sounding small if only to make the deity seem bigger. He imagined him as a great bearded figure in flowing robes who possessed awesome power and who could affect life and the world and any person in any home anywhere by nodding or pointing or snapping his fingers, and the nature of the boy's praying acknowledged this: just loud enough to be heard in Heaven, but not so loud that he'd draw attention to himself.

But on this occasion, the boy spoke to God in a way he hadn't before. Standing in his crease, he stared at a point in the grey-blue sky above the bungalow rooftops and he reasoned with God, bartered with him, spoke with him through the warm plastic shell of his mask as if he were a lawyer or a magistrate. He told God that if he would help him stop Roscoe on the penalty shot, he would tell everyone that it was God's work. He would say that the creator or the maker or the almighty—the boy had heard God called all of these things on televised Sunday morning religious shows—had made him stop the person he hated more than anyone else in the world who would grow up to be a terrible person and who would more than likely spread evil the way Hitler or child molesters or thieves or murderers had. He wasn't sure how he would communicate this message, only that he would. He promised God; promised him over and over. He also told him that maybe one day he would even write about this in a book, although who knew when this would happen or if anyone would ever want to read it.

Roscoe stood ten feet in front of the net in the dead middle of the street. The boy thought he seemed maybe a little less intimidating, if only because he was as tired as everyone else, his shoulders stooped and his face weary and burned pale red from the cold. Not only that, but the boy hadn't observed him straight on in a long time.

Roscoe had always stood at the corner of the boy's vision; either that or he'd come up from behind, tripping him to the ground or grabbing him sideways. But from where he was now, and set against the front windows and snow-rippled awnings of familiar houses on the boy's street, he looked less like a terrible horrible menace and more like a big ugly kid too awkwardly hulking for his age. Or maybe that wasn't the case at all. Maybe the boy was seeing him this way because God had put the idea in his head. Maybe his prayers were already paying off.

Roscoe moved forward with the ball on his stick. The boy lowered himself into a crouch and waited, coiled, for the bully to make his move. Roscoe—a left-handed shot—swished this way and that way, and then he faked to his right before moving back to his left. Because he was so big and had such a long reach, his stick must have swept four feet across the top of the crease, the boy moving sideways with him. Roscoe lunged to his right and the boy leaned to cover the area, his body tipping like a potted plant being knocked over. Because he was falling Roscoe had room to slide the ball under him, and the thug sensed this as he slung the ball toward the net. The other kids watched standing in the snowbank, their sticks planted like Neptune's tridents in waves of snow.

The boy felt his body hit the ground—it met the street with a hard, flat thump—but, looking out, he saw that Roscoe's footing had betrayed him, slipping on the frozen snow. The bully fell to eye level with the boy as the ball moved past him, striking the far post and skipping into the soft angel cake of the great snowbank, disappearing from view.

Roscoe got up and turned to Jimmy James: "You're fucking dead!" But Jimmy just laughed, running toward the boy with the others. The boy's teammates slapped him on the shoulder, telling him how amazing he was and all of that. Knowing what he was required to do, he said, "No, it wasn't me. It was God who did it." Nobody said anything. The boy wasn't sure they'd heard. Then Johnny reminded everybody that they had to win the game—which they did, 24–23—and the boy forgot to tell them ever again.

25

I tried to scratch in all the right places. I stayed in touch with Yvon Martin and Jim Keon, annoying them with relentless emails. I asked former New York Islander Hall of Famer Bryan Trottier to put a word in for me, and did the same with McKenny and all the other people you've read about so far. Mike Pelyk, a former Leafs defenceman whom I'd interviewed for one of my other books, was the only person not to tell me to press forward. "If Dave doesn't respond to you," he said, "you have no chance. That's just the way he is and, you know, you have to respect that. He doesn't care about his legacy and neither should you."

But I did care. I bought a plane ticket to Florida—West Palm Beach—where I knew Keon lived in a community on a golf course, retired after years of selling real estate. I informed the captain's son and his brother about my intentions. I told Yvon, too. I learned that Keon's wife was a maître d' at a popular local restaurant and that he sometimes ate there, although I told myself that I'd try to resist ambushing him in public. It didn't seem right, and the last thing I wanted was the captain angry—or worse, disappointed—in me, even though I knew it would give my book an ending. Instead, I'd hold out and wait until Keon wanted to see me. And if he didn't want to see me, well, that was okay, too. Endings are rarely how any of us imagine them to be.

A few weeks before I was due to leave for Florida, the NHL and the NHLPA settled their work stoppage, and a few weeks after that, the season started: Leafs versus Habs in Montreal. Despite my confusion and antipathy and resentment toward the team and all they'd wrought on their longstanding fans, I watched the game with my dad and stepmom in their lakeside condo at the western tip of the city. Snow fell on Toronto, the Leafs won convincingly, and those old feelings of hope and possibility returned despite my efforts to keep them pressed into the shadows of my thoughts. Two days later the Maple Leafs were scheduled to face the Buffalo Sabres in the home opener, and I secured a seat in the press box, hoping it might be a chance to get past what had happened to me the last time I was in the rink to see Rush.

On the evening of the game I took the subway from Ossington to Union, where I walked with hundreds of others through the train station to get to the arena standing behind it. One of Ken Dryden's first ideas when building a new rink to replace Maple Leaf Gardens was to put it on top of the station, imagining, in his romantic, Drydenesque way, the great unwashed arriving by locomotive to fulfill their dream of seeing the Leafs play. His vision proved untenable, but there were still traces of romance in the station's rolling train schedule, newsagents selling papers, candy, and gum, tired shift workers sitting on benches dreaming of faraway lives, and hockey fans of every age and size traversing its expanse in a great blue huddle. The cold January air pressed against the south doors of the rink. Like an epic song or the distant footfall of a large beast, the sound of the arena announced its presence with a slow, rising build before, through another set of doors, life and colour exploded.

There were Leafs photos and Dion Phaneuf cutouts and Nazem Kadri ads lining the hallway that connected the station to the rink. A busking violinist—a young mother with a sign propped up in her case reading JUST HAD CHILD NUMBER TWO—played the *Hockey Night in Canada* theme, and something about the famous melody echoing through the hallway busy with voices—Toronto voices, Leafs voices—weakened my heart so that all the emotions of the last few months fell upon me. I thought of the violinist's kids; I thought of my kids; I thought of myself as a kid. I thought about happiness and joy and how hockey was deeply buried within this happiness, my happiness. The Leafs would probably lose the home opener—in fact they *would* lose it, 2–1—and they'd probably lose a ton more games that year, but it was impossible not to feel joyful in that moment, the beginning of a new season seeming more profound after all I'd done in the months leading up to it, even more considering how dreary and defeated I'd felt in the previous campaign. But that was before I'd dealt with my past or found Roscoe or gone in search for my hero, whom I hadn't met, but still. No matter how unfulfilled, the journey had made me feel less sorry for myself as a Leafs fan.

I approached the rink's main concourse past rows of tabletop hockey games, basketball hoops, and video screens showing Leafs goals from then and now. Through the swishing of air hockey paddles and the squeaking of tabletop rods turning players after a small dancing puck, I spared a moment to see if Keon was anywhere in the video reel, and he was, wearing a deep blue 70s sweater and deking Rogie Vachon wide before backhanding the puck into the net. Satisfied that the captain had been recognized in this visual best-of, I made my way toward the entrance to the press box, only to stop a second time, and stop hard. A sweater. KEON. Staring back at me.

The fellow was older and less angry than the kid I'd seen at the bottom of my street. He had salt-and-pepper hair and wore pleated trousers. He was standing by himself, presumably waiting for someone, so I stood there, too. I thought about what it meant to see a Keon sweater on opening night, but then I remembered where seeing the last Keon sweater had got me, which wasn't any closer to my hero. Still, before I moved on, I noticed people pointing at the man's sweater, talking to him, or rather to it.

"Helluva sweater!" "My favourite player!" "He'd come back if he saw that!" and "Number fourteen: the best!" It was extraordinary. The chorus grew thicker as people filed past and the game neared. A man and his son walked by, and, after the father had given the sweater-wearer a thumbs-up, the boy said something to his dad. The man leaned over and you could tell what he was saying. "You see, there was once a player for the Leafs named Dave Keon ..."

I collected my press pass and headed to the elevator that would take me to the sixth floor and press row. A set of elevator doors opened and an older man who stood beside me—tall and wearing a beige baseball cap—moved toward them, only to have them close abruptly. "Guess they don't want me," he joked, feigning sadness. Everyone laughed. George Armstrong could still crack 'em up.

With my press pass slung about my neck, I saw a person I thought I recognized moving past me. I turned to see who it was, and was startled by the face: it was Dave Keon. But, of course, it wasn't. It was his son, nearly the spitting image of his father. The words leapt out of my throat: "Hey, Dave." Dressed in his official navy blue NHL jacket, Keon Jr.'s eyes met mine. "Oh, hey there," he said, recognizing me as well.

I felt strange standing there, an interloper having lived with and explored a story—his father's story—that, while important to me, had been and continued to be part of his life. If I was a writer who thought he knew a thing or two about hockey, Dave Jr. had been born into the game. I started to say something—"I'm sorry for having been such a pain in the ass, but, you know. I still plan on going to Florida to stalk your father"—but he spoke first.

"Listen, I lost your number," he said.

"Oh."

"Will you email it to me?"

"Yeah, of course, sure."

"Because my dad ..." His voice trailed off. "My dad might be coming up here in a few weeks."

"Really?" I asked, witlessly.

"Yeah. Send me your number," he said. "We might be able to arrange something."

26

The boy loved summer, but he loved winter more, although sometimes spring was better than either one—you knew that something was about to change, just not how or when. The changes happened slowly, making you notice them even more. To the boy, the first sign was water pooling on the edges of the driveway where there'd once been only a crust of ice and snow. Then came the sound of his mom on a bright Saturday afternoon going into the old-smelling wardrobe in the basement where she'd stashed the boy's running shoes and windbreaker and rubber boots, making sure they were where they were supposed to be in case the winter thaw happened faster than expected, which it did, and would, every year the boy grew older. Even the sounds outside the boy's bedroom window changed. Car tires that had crunched across the snow now went *splffffffffft,* pinwheeling water along the wet road, and whereas the boy's dog was mostly silent on winter evenings save for the occasional huff or snort coming from the haybed in his outside kennel, by March and April he was moving around in the late hours, snapping at just-born bugs after a season stilled by cold. The changes promised more light, more warmth, but better than that, they promised the playoffs. The Leafs were in. After beating whomever they had to beat and tying a few good teams, they'd salted away the last playoff spot in their division.

Something else happened in the early days of March. The boy had anticipated a renewal of Roscoe's beatings, even more so considering what had happened in the street hockey game. But on the first mild week of the year, Roscoe left him alone.

On Friday morning the boy passed the front of the common to find the bully sitting on another kid, slapping his head and calling him spaz. The boy quickened his pace, his heart pumping great bursts of hope that his nightmare was finally over. Trailing off the grounds toward the intersection inside a mass of other kids, the boy thought he could hear the new victim wail like a baby as Roscoe hit him. He thought about how weak the kid sounded and how he must have been a coward and a wimp. Only farther down the road did the boy realize what it said about him that he'd accepted—even relished—seeing a new doormat getting bullied; that he didn't care it was happening even though he knew these thoughts were the opposite of courage or valour. Still, they came and went without engaging the boy's conscience. He was free and that was all that mattered. Whether that made him a terrible person, he wasn't sure.

A few days before the start of the playoffs, the Leafs beat the Golden Seals again at the Gardens, 5–3. The game was special partly because it was the best game the young centreman, Darryl Sittler, had played as a Leaf— he scored two goals and two assists to lead the Leafs' amazing comeback after being down 3–1—and partly because of the second-period brawl. After all that had happened with Roscoe, it was difficult for the boy to be completely absorbed whenever the Leafs emptied their bench, and even though he liked seeing his favourite team fight, something in his gut told him it was wrong because it meant he condoned what Roscoe was doing to him. Once the beatings stopped, however, it was fun again to shout and get excited whenever Tiger Williams did what he did, which, versus California, was to jump off the bench and hammer Joey Johnston into a bloody pulp after the Seals forward cut Lanny McDonald for seven stitches. Then, after being repaired in the intermission, McDonald started the next period by beating up John Stewart so badly that he had to be taken by ambulance to St. Michael's Hospital with a broken face. The Leafs scored four unanswered goals to win. The playoffs were a few weeks away, and according to Sittler, the team was ready. "You could say we're in fighting trim," he told Bob Goldham on the Global broadcast, trying not to wink at the camera.

Things were going so well with the Leafs that Saturday morning yielded a special treat—a front-page profile of the captain written by Frank Orr: "During the past month, he's been the Keon of old, the flitting, darting centre pestering the other teams when they have the puck and giving them problems when he has it." Keon told the writer that, while the year had been disappointing given the team's slow start, he thought that with a little luck the Leafs could go far in the playoffs against teams like Los Angeles, Pittsburgh, and even the horrible terrible Flyers. The boy agreed with the captain. It could be the Leafs' year.

If the Keon story wasn't enough, there was another cool item on the front page of the *Star*'s sports section: daredevil Evel Knievel was going to appear in the intermission of the WHA's Toronto Toros game, the city's other hockey team that the boy liked but didn't love, at least not the way he loved the Leafs. The boy owned a toy Evel Knievel motorcycle like the kind Knievel had used to try to jump the Snake River Canyon. He would set the tiny bike at the edge of the bed and make it fly off the mattress, only to be rescued from disaster by a built-in parachute, the same as in real life. The story told how too many close calls had made Knievel give up regular daredevilling, and how he was now in the business of "promotions," a word the boy didn't understand, but might have meant doing things in public that didn't involve nearly getting killed as a result. One promotion would happen at the Toros game, where Knievel would earn five thousand dollars for every goal scored against either Les Binkley, Gilles Gratton, or Jim Shaw.

The story also talked about how Knievel had been a

longtime hockey fan and player, once trying out for the
Seattle Totems and the Charlotte Checkers. Knievel—
whose hero was Gordie Howe—told Jim Kernaghan of the
Star how he once robbed the Czechoslovakian Olympic
hockey team's dressing room after promoting a game in
his hometown of Butte, Montana. "He was caught red-
handed," wrote Kernaghan, "with $700 and an assortment
of the players' pocket knives." Why Knievel wanted to rob
the opposing team wasn't explained in the story. But he
was Evel Knievel, the world's greatest daredevil. He could
do whatever he wanted.

Other stories were about how the Toronto Toros had
offered the Soviet Union one million dollars each to acquire
the rights to two Russian players with strange names,
Valeri Kharlamov and Alexander Yakushev; plans for the
Gardens to televise the first game of the Leafs' playoff
series against Los Angeles (the CBC having committed its
airtime to the Academy Awards), setting the price at six
dollars per ticket and featuring live play-by-play by Dave
Hodge; Kings goalie Rogie Vachon's recent adoption of a
Vietnamese child, the only survivor of a recent plane crash
in Saigon; and an item announcing the Ontario Hockey
League's all stars, with Dennis Maruk getting the most
votes over Bruce Boudreau, John Tonelli, Mike Kitchen,
Mark Napier, Doug Jarvis, and Don Edwards.

A few days later there was more Keon news, this
time about his son, Tim, whose picture was in the paper
carrying a small trophy around the rink. Tim was fifteen
and had scored two goals in the BB Division final of the

Timmy Tyke tournament, winning 6−5 in a game refereed by King Clancy and Cal Gardner. Because even the small Keons were having success, the boy took this as a sign—a "foreshadowing" Mrs. Reynolds had once called it—of good things to come for the Leafs, the city, the boy, and his family. Not only that, but Roscoe had found a new victim to beat on. Spring was bringing more change than the boy could have possibly imagined.

It was only after he grew up that the boy learned not to assume anything until it had turned into something, and that not until the first bud had popped and the skies had drained themselves of snow did spring actually bring change. This was especially true in Canada, when winter fell only after a long fight, choking the life out of early flowers and cementing the moist earth into the turbid footpaths of late-April ice. As much as the boy felt sunny and good heading to school that last week in April, Roscoe made certain that he would never again open the bedroom curtains onto an early morning unaware of the season's ruse. "Taking one game at a time" was something that hockey players said a lot, and come spring, it's what the boy would do the rest of his life, weathering April and May before embracing the freedom of June or July. Mrs. Reynolds had once said "Beware the Ides of March." That probably meant something too.

It was the worst beating yet: vengeful, unrelenting, and longer than those that had come before. After it was over, the boy dragged his broken-zippered Adidas bag home through late-for-dinner darkness, moving at a kicked-dog's pace, sore, foul, and wet. Walking into the dreadful sound of knives and forks being scraped across plates, the boy doubled over like a crooked stovepipe, moving down the hallway saying that he felt like throwing up before heading to the safety of the bathroom. His mother came to the door and asked if he was okay and the boy pushed his face into a towel trying to muffle the sobbing. If he'd felt like a spaz or a gimp or a homo before, he was certainly one now. Not only that, but he was also dumb. Motherfucking dumb. He only thought these words, but he wanted to scream them, to cry them out. After he stopped crying, he said them quietly into the towel. He said them again and again and again. "David, are you okay?" He was going to Hell for sure.

Lying in bed with a towel on his head and a puke bucket at his side—and starving, having not eaten anything—he saw the bully's face in front of him as he pressed the boy against the cold hard brick of the middle-school wall. "Now I'm going to hit you, loser. Hard. Right here in the pit of your stomach. Better not puke," said Roscoe.

"Ready?"

The boy said nothing.

"Ready, browner?"

The boy stood there trying not to cry.

"Okay, here goes!"

Roscoe wound up to hit him—eyes flaring, teeth bared, hair wild and tentacled—but stopped before burying his fist in the boy's stomach.

Anticipating the pain of the blow, the boy lost himself,

exploding with the hot piss of terror that soaked his pants and socks.

Roscoe stood there, laughing and pointing. He moved at him, slapping the boy's head. The boy put up his hands and tried turning away. Roscoe grabbed him, but the boy held his stance. They tangled and fell to the ground. There, the boy used the only weapon he had, the only thing he could have done short of fighting the bully, which he refused to do, even though it's what he wanted to do more than anything. He rolled toward Roscoe and then pressed at him, his piss-soaked legs and waist moving against his.

"Ackkkk! Fuckin' gross!" said Roscoe.

He pressed again at Roscoe, who squirmed away.

"Fuck off!"

The boy kept moving toward the bully. It wasn't until months later that he saw the irony of it all: trying to get closer to someone he'd spent the better part of the year trying to avoid.

"You're fucking sick you sick fucking freak!"

The boy had never thought of himself this way before. He wasn't sick or weird or anything like that. He was normal and Roscoe was a freak; at least that's what he thought. The bully pulled himself to his feet, stained wet with the boy's urine. "Ughhhhh, fuckin' disgusting!" The boy made sure that Roscoe was long gone before he picked his cold, wet, and savaged body off the ground.

The next week brought even more drama, this time on the ice surface of the Boston Garden, where something happened that the boy wouldn't have believed if he hadn't read about it himself: Dave Keon in a fight, the first of his career, against Gregg Sheppard of the Boston Bruins. It came in the last game of the Leafs' 74/75 season, the captain's last regular-season game ever for the team, although of course the boy wouldn't have known that, nor could he ever have imagined it. Measured against other fights—especially those of the era—it signified little beyond the nature of the combatants: a middling Bruins scorer on a good team against one of the most hard-working and gentlemanly players of all time. A few years after the encounter, Keon told the *Toronto Star*: "Sheppard pushed me from behind and, I can't explain why, but it really bothered me. [After the fight] I said to the linesman, John D'Amico: 'John, I don't know what I'm supposed to do.' He just laughed and said, 'Now we all go off to the penalty box. I only got a two-minute penalty, so I guess it wasn't much of a fight.'" After the boy grew to be a man, he met Jim McKenny, one of the defencemen from 74/75. He asked if McKenny thought Dave Keon's fighting in his last regular-season game as a Leaf—the team would start a best-of-three series in Los Angeles in a few days—meant that he knew something was ending. "Nah," McKenny said, waving his hand in front of his face. "He probably just thought, 'I don't mind taking shit, but I'm sure as hell not gonna take it from Gregg fuckin' Sheppard.'"

It was a plausible theory, but the boy as a man wasn't sure. He believed that Keon did what he did partly as a message to Ballard, telling him, "This is what you've driven me to and this is what I'll leave you with." The boy, on the other hand, thought Keon's gesture was meant solely for him, suggesting that no matter how important it was to be good and virtuous and true and kind and well-behaved and respectful in life, sometimes you had to do what you'd sworn you'd never do. What Keon was saying was that it was okay to fight back, even—or especially—against people like Roscoe. God would just have to deal with it whenever the time came.

The boy spent Monday's school day filled with a sense of nauseated dread, not so much for what Roscoe might do to him when and if he fought back, but for how it would all come to pass once he walked out of those middle-school doors at 3:30 p.m. on Monday, April 27, 1975.

Roscoe was waiting for him—arms crossed, one foot storked against the school wall, smiling his crooked evil smile.

The boy tightened his pale fists, scrunched his brow, and moved toward the bully.

"Look out!" shouted Roscoe, laughing and tipping his head back as if sharing a private joke with someone from above (although probably not God). It was this look away that allowed the boy to mount his attack. He ran full speed at Roscoe and drove his head into his midsection, sending him with an *oooooff!* to the ground. Roscoe fell with a thud, suggesting a bulk of baby fat under his belt and on the flank of his thighs. The boy moved to contain him, but Roscoe climbed to his feet. Still the boy lunged at him, forearms landing with full force on his chest cavity. Roscoe expressed sour air into the boy's face, pushed out from the weight of the blow.

Then Roscoe gathered himself and went for the boy's arms, but the boy did the same. For a while they grappled like two seamen fighting to command the wheel of a ship, turning clockwise and then back again. Roscoe tried to trip him but the boy jumped back. They pushed and pulled and *Nrrggggged!* while trying to subdue each other. The boy thought he might spit in Roscoe's face. But, one, it would be the act of a desperate man; two, it would have ruined a pretty decent test of strength; and three, Roscoe, he sensed, was privately thrilled he was fighting back.

Both boys grew tired. The wheel spun out of their hands and their bodies tumbled to the ground. The boy climbed to his feet first, followed by Roscoe. They stood there, panting. Neither said a word.

For the rest of the year and the rest of their lives, this was the last contact they would ever have. The boy would grow up to be a man who, like all men, would reflect on his life, looking for ways to explain who he was and how he'd gotten from one point to the next. He would often return to the moment when he and Roscoe exhaled, swept the dirt off their pants, and walked away. The boy went this way and became one man; Roscoe went that way and became someone else. It was over. Or something was beginning. The boy wasn't sure.

27

"8:30 in the morning. The Royal York Hotel. There's a coffee shop below the lobby. We'll meet there."

The email had come from Dave Keon Jr., explaining that his father was willing to meet me. After reading it, my wife asked me if I was nervous. I told her I wasn't, at least not wholly. Besides, I felt the way most artists feel when they near the final days of their work: grateful to have survived the process and thrilled to see the end— which would come in a few days at the very hotel where Yvon Martin had met Wilf Cude. I made a note to tell Keon Yvon's story; maybe it would be the first thing I'd tell him. Or maybe I'd tell him about the recent passing of the Radio Hotel's former owner, Harry Korman, with whom the captain had played baseball and about whom I'd written a *National Post* column, which a friend of Yvon's had sent to Keon. Or maybe I'd tell him about seeing his house. Or finding his stick in the Rouyn Forum. Or talking to McKenny: what a character he was. Or seeing Rush and not finding his banner and then having a panic attack. Or the torn crest and the Flyers. What happened after school. Gandhi. And how, even though something new had started on the day I fought back, something had ended, too, because Dave Keon would never again be a Maple Leaf and life would always be different. Maybe I was nervous after all.

I awoke early that morning and picked out my clothes as if going to a job interview or court date or important ceremony. Besuited, yet forgoing a tie, I taxied to the hotel twenty minutes early and found a table at York's Deli & Bakery, a cafeteria in the lower level of the hotel. I sat there doing what anyone does while waiting to meet someone important: fidgeting, moving my elbows around on the table, tilting my head this way and that, ordering then reordering things on the table. People came and went and moments passed that felt like hours. And then Keon walked in.

He wore a dark sweater and a white turtleneck, hair shaved close to the skull. He was old, sure, but square-shouldered and steady-moving as he drifted toward the table. Because his eyes—dark, stolid, penetrating—had always been his most compelling feature, it was only after a while that I noticed the worn skin and seventy-something pallor of his face, more noticeable in relief against all the photographs, television images, and old game films transferred to VHS or DVD that I'd absorbed.

He lowered himself into his chair across from me, his son sitting at his elbow to his right.

When he first spoke, I had to lean in to hear him. His voice was a little thin and quieter than I'd remembered, but this could have been owing to the din of the room. Since I was keyed to every word, it wasn't long before I heard him perfectly. He closed his hands on the table, opening them only after his son put a coffee and blueberry muffin down in front of him.

I began by asking him whether Wilf Cude had had a fighting chance in attempting to persuade Mrs. Keon to let him go to Hamilton instead of St. Mike's, a question that saw the two men turn to each other and laugh, which I took to be a positive beginning. Next, we talked about Harry Korman—how Keon had played softball for him, and how Rouyn-Noranda had once relied heavily on the hotelier as a sporting booster. I asked the captain if he'd read the story I'd written about his friend. He said that he had. After gathering some courage I asked him what he thought, and he told me, nodding his head, "It was very good." I heard myself exhale, and the rest of conversation carried on like a dream.

We talked for an hour and a half. If there was a sense among former teammates and some writers that Keon had grown into a disenchanted old man, I didn't see it. He was warm and easy to talk to. Even when discussing the 1970s Flyers, he showed tremendous grace and respect for a team that didn't deserve it. "A lot of what they did," he said, "overshadowed the fact that there were some great players on that team, players like Reggie Leach." Which made me want to tell him about Roscoe, but I didn't. Not yet.

The captain addressed all my questions as if unconcerned about saying the wrong thing or giving the wrong impression. If any inquiry was too strong, he'd look at his son and they'd roll their eyes, then laugh some more. A few times the son made fun of his dad, and sometimes the father gave it back. I asked whether, before his bout with Gregg Sheppard, he'd ever been tempted to fight. Both men slammed their hands on the table and looked to the skies.

"Oh, all the time," said Keon.

"That's assuming you could call what happened in Boston a fight," said the son.

"Did you fight because of what had happened during that year?" I asked. "Did you do it because of Harold Ballard and all he'd put you through?"

Keon passed a hand through the air. "No, it wasn't anything like that," he said. "It just kind of happened, although, you know, not much really happened."

"Maybe it's like what McKenny said," I told him.

"What did he say?"

"He said, 'Davey probably thought, 'I don't mind taking shit, but I'm sure as hell not going to take it from Gregg fuckin' Sheppard.'"

Keon laughed. "I can't believe McKenny can remember anything, let alone something that happened that year."

I nodded in agreement, thinking that because I'd sworn in the captain's company, we were now having a real conversation. A hockey conversation. And that's what we fuckin' did.

The captain told me about the Keon-Harris hockey school ("Paul Coffey and Tom Laidlaw went there," he said proudly); growing up in Rouyn-Noranda ("Our house was so small and crowded I couldn't wait to get down to the rink"); his father's love of hockey ("He was passionate and he thought he knew everything about the game," he said, laughing); working in the mines ("All of our parents worked there, and they wanted something better for their kids; that's why a lot of my friends went to school"); the last days in the life of Spinner Spencer ("I'd talked with him on the phone before he died, but no, I was not asked to identify the body"); and how Wilf Cude had played in Melville before coming to the NHL, the sound of his voice saying the name of one of my spiritual homes becoming stuck evermore in the needle groove of my thoughts.

Not wanting to ruin a good time but feeling obliged to pose the question, I asked how he felt about team ceremonies and other events that celebrated his achievements. He sighed a little—sounding more tired than exasperated, I thought—and said, "Well, I'm just not interested." I was about to expound on what a sweater-raising ceremony would mean to the essence of the Leafs' future and how being honoured in the new rink would be the natural result of our encounter, but decided against it. I was finally in the presence of my hero. The sporting universe could do whatever it wanted with it.

I asked him about Bobby Baun's story about the Leafs watching Keon play in Rouyn-Noranda, but the captain said it wasn't true; they'd come for training camp after he'd left for St. Mike's. I told him that, in Baun's book, the team had gone to the Radio Hotel to see Stompin' Tom, and he said that sounded about right.

"We used to see him play in Peterborough too, whenever we had training camp up there," he said.

"Do you think Baun is maybe confusing his stories?" I asked.

"He may be," he said. "Although Tom was in the north back then. Do you know how he was discovered?" I told him that I didn't think I did, even though I knew every detail of how Tom Connors walked into the Maple Leaf Hotel with thirty-five cents in his pocket—five cents shy of a beer—and earned the remaining money after playing a few songs in the corner for the barkeep. I also knew that he stayed for fourteen months and that the shows jump-started his career, but still, I sat listening to the voice of one legend describe the origin myth of another, a ley line borne across Formica and muffin crumbs right there in the basement of Canada's most famous hotel.

We paused to sip our coffees. Then Keon shuffled in his seat a little, slid his elbow across the table, and leaned forward. He asked me, "So what exactly are you doing?"

I drew in a breath. Then I told him everything you've just read, distilling the entirety of my life into a five-minute confessional while looking into the eyes of my hero, who looked back, not saying anything, just listening, his hands once again folded on the table.

The captain remained quiet for a moment. Then he said, "Thank you."

"No, thank you," I told him.

We fell quiet once again.

"So you've been a Leafs fan for a long time," he said.

"Yes," I told him. "Ever since I was a boy."

AUTHOR'S NOTE

The inspiration for *Keon and Me* was born out of the song "Fourteen and Me," written by my friend and Morningstar teammate Stephen Stanley for the "Stolen from a Hockey Card" concert in Charlottetown, PEI, in 2012. I owe a great debt to the Keon family and the people of Rouyn-Noranda; everyone at Quebec Tourism; my exceptional agent, Sam Haywood, and my wise and compassionate editor, Nick Garrison of Penguin Canada (not forgetting the work of Karen Alliston and Mary Ann Blair); the Toronto Maple Leafs and Pat Park; CBC's Q and the *National Post*; a few friends who helped read the work; and, of course, my family. Parts of the storytelling in this book, my twelfth, have been disguised or corrupted for the more personal sections. Also, timelines have been slightly shuffled and names changed wherever required. Most of the prose remains as true to non-fiction as possible, if toeing the waters of what some experts have taken to calling "creative non-fiction." (I know: exciting, right?) Should you take issue with this or any other element of this book—or even if you just like it—please find me @hockeyesque or at davebidini@gmail.com. Also, Anne Garfield may have favoured apple pie, rather than blueberry. Sometimes, memory betrays even the most vital details.